BUCKNELL REVIEW

Perspectives on Contemporary Spanish American Theatre

STATEMENT OF POLICY

BUCKNELL REVIEW is a scholarly interdisciplinary journal.
Each issue is devoted to a major theme or movement in the humanities or sciences, or to two or three closely related topics. The
editors invite heterodox, orthodox, and speculative ideas and welcome manuscripts from any enterprising scholar in the humanities and sciences.

This journal is a member of the Conference of Editors of Learned Journals

BUCKNELL REVIEW
A Scholarly Journal of Letters, Arts, and Sciences

Editor
PAULINE FLETCHER

Associate Editor
DOROTHY L. BAUMWOLL

Assistant Editor
STEVEN W. STYERS

Contributors should send manuscripts with a self-addressed
stamped envelope to the Editor, Bucknell University, Lewisburg,
PA, 17837.

BUCKNELL REVIEW

Perspectives on Contemporary Spanish American Theatre

Edited by
FRANK DAUSTER

Lewisburg
Bucknell University Press
London: Associated University Presses

Associated University Presses
440 Forsgate Drive
Cranbury, NJ 08512

Associated University Presses
16 Barter Street
London WC1A 2AH, England

Associated University Presses
P.O. Box 338, Port Credit
Mississauga, Ontario,
Canada L5G 4L8

The paper used in this publication meets the
requirements of the American National Standard for
Permanence of Paper for Printed Library Materials Z39.48-1984.

(Volume XL, Number 2)

ISBN 0-8387-5345-0
ISSN 0007-2869

PRINTED IN THE UNITED STATES OF AMERICA

Contents

Recent Issues of BUCKNELL REVIEW

Notes on Contributors

Jacqueline Eyring Bixler is associate professor of Spanish at Virginia Polytechnic Institute. She has published a number of essays on the theatre of Emilio Carballido and other Latin American dramatists. She is currently finishing a book titled *Convention and Transgression: The Theatre of Emilio Carballido*.

Ronald D. Burgess is a professor of Spanish at Gettysburg College. His major research interest is contemporary Mexican theatre. He has published several articles and a book, *The New Dramatists of Mexico, 1967–1985*.

Sandra Messinger Cypess is professor of Spanish at the University of Maryland. She is author of numerous essays on Latin American drama and Hispanic women writers in journals in the United States and Latin America, a review essay on twentieth-century Latin American theatre to be published by Cambridge University Press, and *La Malinche in Mexican Literature: From History to Myth*. Her current research deals with mother images in the configuration of Mexican national identity.

Frank Dauster is professor emeritus of Spanish at Rutgers the State University of New Jersey. His most recent book is *Perfil generacaional del teatro hispanoamericano (1894–1924): Chile, México, El Río de la Plata*. He is currently working on a study of contemporary Mexican poets.

William García is instructor in Spanish at Union College. He is finishing his doctoral dissertation on the subversion of classical tragedy in Spanish American theatre.

Priscilla Meléndez is associate professor of Spanish at The Pennsylvania State University where her major interests are Spanish American theatre and Mexican and Caribbean literature. Her *La dramaturgia hispanoamericana contemporánea: teatralidad y autoconciencia* was published in 1990 and she is presently finishing a book entitled *Farce and Falsehood in Spanish American Theatre.*

KIRSTEN F. NIGRO is associate professor of Spanish at the University of Cincinnati. She is review editor of the *Latin American Theatre Review* and was guest editor for the special issue on Modern Mexican Theatre (Spring 1985). She has published numerous essays on theatre in journals in the United States and Latin America and edited *Palabras más que comunes,* essays on José Triana. Her study of Vicente Leñero's *Nadie sabe nada* appeared in *Essays in Honor of Frank Dauster* which she co-edited with Sandra Cypess.

PETER ROSTER is professor and chair of Spanish at Carleton University. He has done extensive editorial and bibliographical work in Latin American theatre. He is the author of *La ironía como método de análisis literario: La poesía de Salvador Novo* and co-author of *Bibliografía del teatro hispanoamericano contemporáneo.* He is presently working on the history of twentieth-century Argentine and Chilean theatre.

DIANA TAYLOR is professor of Spanish and Comparative Literature and director of the theatre group Primer Acto at Dartmouth College. Her *Theatre in Crisis: Drama and Politics in Latin America* received several awards, and she is also the author of the forthcoming *Disappearing Acts: Spectacles of Gender and Nationalism in Argentina's "Dirty War."* She has edited and co-edited five volumes of essays on theatre in Spanish and written widely on Latino and Latin American theatre and performance.

GEORGE WOODYARD is professor of Spanish at the University of Kansas where he has held several administrative positions and currently serves as dean of international studies. As founder and editor of the *Latin American Theatre Review,* he has devoted his scholarly interests to the theatre and has been instrumental in the development of the field as an academic discipline. He has also written on the theatre of Chile, Argentina, and Mexico, and edited the complete works of Egon Wolff.

Introduction:
Contemporary Spanish American
Theatre

WITHIN an academic world characterized in recent decades by the proliferation of critical and theoretical stances, Spanish American literature is remarkable in that this vitality extends to the creative literatures themselves. Poetry in Spanish America today is the heir to a long tradition of distinguished poets; although only Sor Juana Inés de la Cruz among earlier authors is widely known in the non-Spanish-speaking world, Nobel awards to Pablo Neruda and Octavio Paz and the recognition of leading feminine voices like Rosario Castellanos or the poets of social commitment like Ernesto Cardenal have generated considerable interest in the United States. In the same way, the years since the explosion of the boom in the 1960s have made of Carlos Fuentes, José Donoso, Mario Vargas Llosa, and Gabriel García Márquez, among many others, frequent visitors to American university campuses and recipients of honors, subjects of symposia, and frequent names on the best-sellers lists. These phenomena and the emergence or revitalization of subdisciplines such as colonial studies have changed the face of criticism in the subject.

Almost unnoticed by the non-Spanish-speaking audiences is the fact that theatre has experienced a boom equally startling and equally vital. It is no longer limited to the heroic endeavors of a few committed souls in major cities; there are more or less ongoing seasons in every substantial city, fueled in large measure by university-based schools of drama. The theatre was a major component of the protests against tyranny in Chile and Argentina; it has become an organ of dissident voices throughout the deprived urban slums and indigenous communities. Its dramatists are conversant with the latest of international drama and founded the largely autochthonous movement of collective creation; many groups have absorbed the rituals and even the mythology of the non-Hispanic communities. In the United States, theatre, in both

11

English and Spanish, has become a potent voice in the struggle of Hispanic Americans against racial and social discrimination.

The surge in interest in Spanish American theatre over the last few decades and the merely scattered interest prior to that have meant that with the exception of a few investigators working largely independently, there was no preexisting community of interest within which younger scholars could develop. There were no American or European academic journals devoted to Latin American theatre, and existing journals were, to say the least, skeptical about this apparent new arrival. (The fact that there were major authors creating important theatre in several Spanish American cities since the late nineteenth century was lost on them.) Almost the only centralized source for information was the *Handbook of Latin American Studies.*

Happily, this situation is totally altered. There are now prestigious academic journals such as *Latin American Theatre Review* and *Gestos,* and it is common to find materials in the field in virtually any academic publication. Instead of the few solitary specialists noted above, with the infrequent opportunity to teach theatre, courses in the subject are included in the basic curriculum of most major colleges and universities. There is a nucleus of active critics based in universities and producing criticism of a high level; there are regular conferences and symposia, often attracting authors and critics from Latin America and Europe, and within the last decade the phenomenon has begun to appear in Mexico, Chile, Argentina, Puerto Rico, and several European nations, including France and Germany. The participants are, as a group, relatively young; even the most senior among them can be expected to continue productivity for a long time to come.

This euphoric picture does, of course, have its down side. The crisis in American public education and the economic problems of the Latin American nations have seriously affected funding for the symposia, which are an integral part of dealing with theatre, providing a large audience with performances which would otherwise require constant major international travel. Not the least of difficulties is the concomitant cutback in faculty positions, with the resulting difficulties in placing the many eager and talented graduate students who flock to theatre studies. Along with these serious and distressing problems are others, less grievous although often frustrating: the simple difficulty of keeping up with a field which is burgeoning far beyond the expectations of anyone connected with it, the exploding bibliographical situations, etc.

The essays in this issue of the *Bucknell Review* have not been selected to provide geographical or methodological coverage, which would in any event be impossible, given the scope of the field. Instead, leading scholars were asked to write something they would *like* to write on the subject of interest, without restrictions other than space. The list of subjects is intriguing: tragedy and marginality, the nature of comedy, metatheatre and parody, the role of women in theatre, myth and metatheatre, role shifting, the parodic demythologizing of the past, the use of classical subjects to interpret the problems of the present. And always, explicitly or implicitly, the profoundly sad social context. If some well-known names and regions are missing, it is the result of the authors' interests in specific subjects at this point in time. Obviously genre and gender are operative words: comedy, tragedy, metatheatre, and the conflictive roles of the sexes in theatre and society. Behind these theoretical examinations and intricately interwoven with them lies a constant of Spanish American literature in recent decades: the reexamination of a past that is not what figures in the official pronouncements.

Priscilla Meléndez's "Co(s)mic Conquest in Sabina Berman's *Aguila o sol*" examines the iconoclastic manner in which Berman not only demythologizes the Spanish Conquest of Mexico and parodies official history while deflating previous dramatic versions—themselves often parodic or demythologizing—but also questions the nature in which theatre approaches or can approach questions of supposed historical truth. This is a particularly relevant point in dealing with Mexico, given the present widespread rejection of the myth of the Revolution, and Meléndez's title with its clear intertextual allusion to Octavio Paz, one of the most persistent critics of the status quo, opens complicated avenues for interpretation.

The fascination that the Conquest holds for Mexican dramatists and their varied ways of dealing with it is seen in Sandra Cypess's "Myth and Metatheatre: Magaña's Malinche and Medea." Where Berman finds the "Truth" behind the story uncapturable, Sergio Magaña sees the ideology of the narrator as a determining factor in the formation of the story. At the same time, he resorts to classical myth to provide a framework for a history which is incapable of being pinned down to facts but which at the same time in some way repeats itself: the Conquest with its litany of betrayal is somehow also Tlatelolco.

The important, if often undervalued, role of women in Mexican theatre—and in all theatre in Latin America—is seen in Kirsten Nigro's examination of the varieties of feminist commitment in the work of three women dramatists: Estela Leñero, Sabina Berman, and Astrid Hadad, whose works range from realism through satire to performance art. Whether on the fringes or operating within the confines of commercial theatre, such artists have added a significant new dimension to Mexican theatre. Ronald Burgess agrees that women are taking the lead in the new theatre in his study of what he calls "bad girls and good boys," that is, the opening of new doors to changing gender roles and alternative sexual preferences in a heavily traditional and male-dominated society. He sees in this opening the source of a recent revival of theatre in Mexico.

The widespread return to classical myth and drama in an effort to express the complex realities of Spanish America is again visible in Diana Taylor's study of Gambaro's *Antígona furiosa*. Although largely based on Sophocles' original, Gambaro's version is clearly specific to the Argentine "Dirty War" and the role of the mothers of the Plaza de Mayo in bringing the generals down. At the same time it is a deliberate rewriting of the myth to make central the role of Antigone, a centralizing of the role of woman in a traditionalist society. In "The Theatre of Roberto Cossa: A World of Broken Dreams" George Woodyard approaches the Argentine situation from a different perspective. Cossa works within the tradition of the ethical realism of Arthur Miller tempered by the Argentine *grotesco* with its legacy of black humor and sociopolitical commentary. Cossa's characters are frustrated, malcontented, and unable to work for a common good, and his plays are increasingly political while remaining profoundly nostalgic.

The movement toward transnational comparative studies is visible in Peter Roster's "Metatheatre and Parody in the Generation of 1924" where he compares the Argentine Roberto Arlt and the Mexican Xavier Villaurrutia, two dramatists normally regarded as drastically different one from the other. But Roster finds basic similarities in the commitment to revitalizing the theatre and the skillful manipulation of exhausted dramatic situations to create new modes of dramatic expression. The last two essays are genre studies, an approach which is becoming increasingly important. Jacqueline Bixler studies the evolution of the form in Emilio Carballido's work, from his first hit in 1950 to *Rosa de dos aromas* in the mid-1980s. At the same time she sees a development in the social attitudes expressed toward a greater emphasis on feminine self-reliance and growing independence. Finally, William García examines Latin American versions of Medea, focusing then on José Triana's transgression of the myth in *Medea en el espejo* with its incorporation of materials from outside the tradition. Again, as in every case, the presence of the sociopolitical subtext is striking. Had there been room and time sufficient to include examinations of other dramatists, to broaden the scope of the volume, we would have found differences, but underneath the same constants are there: the ongoing revision of the tradition, the rapidly growing incorporation of new themes, methods, subjects, the expanding role of women both as subject and as author within a theatre in constant change.

FRANK DAUSTER
RUTGERS UNIVERSITY

BUCKNELL REVIEW

Perspectives on Contemporary Spanish American Theatre

Co(s)mic Conquest in Sabina Berman's *Aguila o sol*

Priscilla Meléndez
The Pennsylvania State University

To John W. Kronik

> El tiempo, que atenúa los recuerdos, agrava el del Zahir. Antes, yo me figuraba el anverso y después el reverso; ahora, veo simultáneamente los dos.
> —Jorge Luis Borges, "El Zahir"

> If we think of modernism as a struggle to make ourselves at home in a constantly changing world, we will realize that no mode of modernism can ever be definitive. Our most creative constructions and achievements are bound to turn into prisons and white sepulchres that we, our children, will have to escape or transform if life is to go on.
> —Marshall Berman, *All That Is Solid Melts into Air*

THERE is an explicit convergence between the Mexican playwright Sabina Berman's *Aguila o sol* (1984) and both historical and documentary theatre. But this convergence flies in the face of characteristics and themes of the work that seem at first glance to be incongruent with a traditionally historicist perspective. An explicit dialogue is established in Berman's play between the conflictive perception of Mexico's past and present and the way in which these two time periods have been dramatized. This dialogue is established by, for example, the grotesque and caricaturizing vein in *Aguila o sol,* the popularizing and anachronistic lens through which the past is seen, the lesser-known version of those who were conquered, and, as a result, a carnivalesque dehistoricization of the Spanish Conquest.

19

Ironically, and on an obvious level, Berman's drama seems to take up once again the well-explored theme of the Conquest and to resort to that skepticism about official Mexican history already dramatized by important and canonical playwrights such as Rodolfo Usigli, Celestino Gorostiza, Salvador Novo, Sergio Magaña, Carlos Fuentes, Emilio Carballido, and Vicente Leñero, among others.[1] This obsessive dramatization of the Mexican past has been widely recognized by critics. Sandra Cypess remarks: "Deconstructing national history in Mexican theatre has served as an important technique, especially in relation to themes concerning the Mexican Revolution, the empire of Maximilian and Carlota, and recently, the Conquest and the 1968 uprising at Tlatelolco" ("CC," 494). Nevertheless, in many of the contemporary works that explore historical questions—whether the exploration of the period of the Conquest, the transculturation and christianization of the indigenous population, the wars of independence during the early decades of the nineteenth century, the so-called period of reformist law of the mid-century, the Second Empire, the Revolution of 1910, or the war of the Cristeros—the protagonists of these dramas are often transformed into emblems of the Mexican present, and much less into careful explorations and redefinitions of historical figures and events.[2]

In many cases, the works of these dramatists represent an effort to recover important figures who have been ignored, or attempt to impart a sense of national pride and unity to the public via historical recreation, or display the antagonistic posture assumed by much of contemporary Mexican theatre with respect to official history, or even try to explain the present.[3] Even in these cases, however, such postures imply processes of substitution and reevaluation that can turn into discourses just as authoritarian, or at least categorical, as those they are attempting to displace or criticize.

Kirsten Nigro, Sandra Cypess, and Jacqueline Bixler have published lucid critical essays on, respectively, rhetoric and history in Mexican dramaturgy, the feminist perspective on construction and revision of the colonial past, and Mexican theatre's discrediting of official history.[4] In these essays, they reveal the consciously and unconsciously deceptive character of many of those twentieth-century Mexican dramatic texts that deal with historical questions. In other words, these three critics insist on the capacity and, at the same time, the limits of these texts to question, explore, and propose multiple and even contradictory visions of the past as well as of their own historical present. For Cypess, a central

example of the limitations of many of these dramas that explore
Mexican history and historiography is their lack of interest in
the exclusion of women: "The male dramatists who began to investigate the validity of the received history have not explored
problems attendant with gender-determined exclusions from historical discourse that the women dramatists now bring on stage"
("CC," 494).[5] Nigro offers another fundamental example of the
limitations of certain contemporary Mexican dramas based on
history when she reveals the antagonistic readings produced by
texts such as Gorostiza's *La Malinche,* Novo's *Cuauhtémoc,* and
Usigli's *Corona de fuego.* On the one hand, and from the perspective of the present, these works represent an affirmation of the
conservative ideology perpetuated by the discredited revolutionary myth of Mexico as a democratic, mixed-race, and united nation. On the other hand, according to Nigro, these three dramas
can also be interpreted as a negative or, at least, ironic vision of
the present and of the inconsistencies of the Revolution ("RH,"
71). But the true limitation results not from a possible duality of
interpretation, but from the lack of awareness in the texts themselves of such a duality.

For this reason it can be said, with due respect for the diversity
of Mexican drama, that the singularity of *Aguila o sol* within the
context of Mexican theatre and its exploration of its own origins
resides in the fact that Berman's play does not seek only to unmask
the contradictory other side of previous versions. Nor does it seek
to be a mere attack on official historiography, nor to understand
its historical present. Rather, it proposes a vision in which the
coin is still in the air, in which the either/or choice between eagle
and sun is not resolved. Or, it can be said that it is resolved, as
Borges would say in "El Zahir," in the possibility of seeing both
sides of the coin at the same time.[6] It could even be said, with
a degree of ironic humor and iconoclastic spirit, that Mexican
dramatists have seen the Borgesian Zahir, that coin which pos-
sesses the awful virtue of making the Mexican past something
obsessive and unforgettable, "whose image ends up driving people mad" ("Z," 110). For Berman, this obsession with history, this
urgency to look into origins, to focus constantly on the same images, must be dismantled in a way specific to these obsessions.
That is, it must be dismantled via the parodic representation of
that castrating and perturbing past, and, of course, from the point
of view of the conquered.

The triple irony that *Aguila o sol* proposes is to emphasize not
only its ability to transgress official history and, at the same time,

to dismantle the version of the vanquished, but to do this by a rigorous calling into question of the verbal and theatrical codes which, in addition to being vehicles of attack, are vehicles by which the codes are themselves attacked. For example, the farcical and popular version of the conquest of Mexico offered by the comedians in *Aguila o sol* provokes a tension between the "laughable" and the grotesque, which is embodied in the indecency, violation, rape, and humiliation to which the indigenous population—in no way homogenous—was subjected.[7] The plural transgressive character of the work shows that the play not only tries to offer an alternative version of history in which the defeated attempt to be vindicated, but also that such an alternative version is also capable of denouncing the contradictions of language and of theatrical structures. The act of taking theatre into the street—which in traditional terms could be considered an act of physical as well as metaphorical dismantling—represents in *Aguila o sol* precisely the transgression of the mode of communication. That is, it is a transgression of theatre as an institution, which is attacked with the same arms it uses to dismantle and to transgress history and historiography.

I intend to show, then, how *Aguila o sol* sets forth and at the same time denounces the illusory vindicative role that theatrical discourse proposes to play with respect to the history of the Conquest. I have pointed out that, by resorting to a theatre based on history, Berman seems to participate in the twentieth-century Mexican theatrical tradition of investigating the Mexican past and present from various ideological perspectives. In *Aguila o sol* the historic past is certainly questioned and caricatured. What is less obvious, but more pertinent for this analysis, is the recognition that theatre, in spite of being the vehicle of communication that unmasks and parodies history, is itself attacked. In other words, in *Aguila o sol* theatre is subjected to a rigorous process of dismantling that aims to denounce its ambiguous and contradictory history. It is sometimes a vehicle of control and at other times an unconscious instrument of its inconsistent communication strategies.

It should be said that Linda Hutcheon indirectly points out this double strategy of deconstruction of both historical and theatrical discourse, although her study of the poetics of postmodernism focuses particularly on an examination of narrative. By defining the concept of "historiographic metafiction" Hutcheon casts implicit light on certain aspects of Berman's theatre, especially on the plural and contradictory historical, linguistic, and theatrical focuses of *Aguila o sol*: "By this [historiographic metafiction] I mean those well-known and popular novels which are both intensely self-reflexive and yet paradoxically also lay claim to historical events and personages."[8]

The caricaturizing stance adopted with respect to all historical events and to the verbal construction of *Aguila o sol* foregrounds the metaphorical level of theatrical language—use of dialogue, scenic composition, histrionic elements, wardrobe, proxemic, kinesic, pictorial, and musical codes—by turning it into a vehicle and a target of criticism.[9] It is through this reflection on the act of communication that the work dramatizes the paradoxical, fragmentary and anticategorizing nature of the verbal and theatrical construction it creates. By means of a blatant exploitation of historical themes and an obvious questioning of Mexican historiography, it unmasks the implicit and ambiguous power of theatrical communication and structures.

In Cypess's aforementioned essay on feminist perspectives in the revision of the colonial past, she has already recognized the internal tension that the work provokes at both the stylistic and the thematic level: "Berman creates a 'mestizo' or heterogenous style by mixing social realism, surrealism techniques, street theatre, satire, and farce. The lack of totalizing form is not a flaw, but one of the drama's important characteristics, revealing the conflicts at the heart of the enterprise of the conquest itself, as well as the subsequent national identity forged by the colonial power" ("CC," 499). Within this framework in which opposites openly coexist, one recognizes too how the dual and contradictory nature of historical as well as linguistic and theatrical reality is highlighted in the "tragicomic" representation of a bloody event in Mexican history.

Before examining Berman's possible motives for leaving the coin suspended in the air or investigating the possible meaning of this transgressive act, it is necessary to make clear what it is that I do not address. I refrain here from exhaustive exploration of fundamental aspects of *Aguila o sol* such as the fascinating contrast between the primary sources (the *Códice Florentino* and the *Lienzo de Tlaxcala*) and the parodical version of the Conquest, or details of the political infighting among Tlaxcaltecs, Cholultecs, and Aztecs, or the multiple sociopolitical meanings incarnated in the figure of La Malinche, or the explicitly farcical nature of the work, or even the grotesque sexual allusions that characterize the drama. From a critical perspective, I intend to enlarge upon those few but perceptive studies of *Aguila o sol* that have examined some of these topics in detail. Jeanne Gillespie, for example, offers a thorough analysis of the pictorial and narrative texts on which Berman bases her play, and which she incorporates into her dramatization of the Conquest. Cypess, on the other hand, emphasizes how Castellanos's *El eterno femenino* and Berman's *Aguila o sol* establish their own reality as (partial) readings of important Mexican historical events from the perspective of those who have been marginalized in that society: women and Indians ("CC," 495).[10]

Aguila o sol, in *Teatro de Sabina Berman* (1985), begins with a brief preface in which the Mexican author acknowledges her debt to the indigenous chronicles collected by Miguel León Portilla in his *Visión de los vencidos* (1959), makes clear her intentional lack of fidelity to a reconstruction of events, and announces the symbolic character of the theatrical devices which she employs. After the preface, the action begins with the song of a mariachi accompanied by a chorus. In his ballad, the mariachi narrates the obscure Indian portents about the arrival of the Spaniards, who are immediately confused with the return of Quetzalcoatl, the fair, white, and bearded god. In turn, these premonitions are represented in the appearance of La Llorona (a mother who has lost her children), in the sudden presence of a bird of ill omen, in the visions of Moctezuma, and in a character without ears who has seen strange beings (fair, white ones). In contrast with this tragic vision of the events to come, we see subsequently that the narration of the Conquest will be in the hands of street comedians surrounded by spectators who applaud and laugh at the story of the outrage, thus imparting to the work the character of a circus show (*AS,* 240–42).

Meanwhile, the meeting between Cortés and the emissaries of Moctezuma (a tiger man, a captive warrior, and two wise men) turns out to be a charade in which the speeches of the conquistador are incoherent and absurd. Nevertheless, the presence of La Malinche permits communication not only between Cortés and the indigenous representatives, but, ironically, between Cortés and the Spanish-speaking audience of the work.[11] The messengers return to tell Moctezuma of the grotesque encounter with the strange beings, and he must decide whether to confront them or to hide on a hill with his wise men in order to protect the knowledge they have amassed (*AS,* 238). Here, Moctezuma recognizes the fragile and transitory nature of his existence. However, before the dramatization of his defeat and death, the first vestiges of betrayal are seen in the massacre at Cholula, where the Tlaxcaltecs ally themselves with the Spanish to defeat the Cholultecs. In addition, the dismemberment of the family of Ixtlixuchitl takes place when his mother refuses to be baptized into the Catholic faith. After a series of scenes in which Moctezuma yields his power to that of the Spaniards, and they greedily and grotesquely seize the Aztec treasures, he dies a humiliating death in very ambiguous circumstances: does he die because he is struck by a stone thrown by an Indian, or because "Cortés stuck a sword up his ass" (*AS*, 264)? As will be shown below, all these scenes occur within the context of a farcical drama, of a performance in which we hear the fusion and confusion of the voices of the narrator, the protagonists and the antagonists, the betrayers and the betrayed— who at a given moment may be mariachis or street comedians or wise men or a chorus or Cortés or Moctezuma. In the final analysis, *Aguila o sol* enacts both the parodic character of historical symbols and events, and of linguistic construction by means of a theatrical language that is fragmented, vulgar, iconoclastic, circuslike, and pantomimic. This theatrical language deflates official history, the reverse of this history, and the communicative process.

It is in this context of contradictions, negations, and transgressions that the importance of the title of Berman's work becomes clear. It alludes to a well-known children's game in which a coin is thrown into the air and the players try to guess which side will show after it falls: the eagle or the sun. For Gillespie, the idea of chance expressed in the title is precisely what opens the way in the work for the satirical treatment of the Conquest: "By suggesting that the outcome of this history is a 50–50 call, Berman establishes the inability of presenting the 'ultimate reality' of these events. Berman's intent, clearly specified in the prologue and insinuated in the title, is not a 'factual' reconstruction of the events but a satirical interpretation generated from the pro-indigenous texts" ("PC," 2). To a certain degree, the obsessive search for national and cultural identity that characterizes Mexican art and thought, and the calling into question of the Mexican philosophical and linguistic makeup, translate into deliberate uncertainty and instability. The much-desired unity of Mexico is represented precisely through historical, ethnic, and social breakup, which seems closer to "reality" than the multiple masks that historical discourse and theatre itself have worn until now.

But, ironically, the initial sensation that one is dealing with a world impregnated with doubt and governed by mere chance disappears, or at least weakens, when one recognizes that—in contrast with the homonymous title of Octavio Paz's text, which contains question marks: *¿Aguila o sol?*—Berman's title has no question marks. Instead, her title presents the choice between the two sides of the coin not as a query but as a categorical answer to the prevalence of doubt.[12] That is, the conjunction *o* [or] does not seem to express a doubtful reality here; rather, it affirms doubt—categorically. It is not a case, then, of answering the question of whether the coin will come up eagle or sun after it has been tossed into the air. It is not a case of seeing if the balance of history will lean fortuitously toward the triumph of the Spaniards or toward the reevaluation of the role of indigenous groups. It is rather a case of stressing how the work itself offers a singular and paradoxical answer that suggests that both historical and theatrical reality *are* at once "eagle or sun." These realities reveal, in other words, their unity and their plurality simultaneously. The image of the coin suspended in the air calls into question not only the multiple interpretations of the Conquest but also the other side of these interpretations. From this perspective of simultaneous unity and diversity, one recognizes the symbolic nature of one of the characters in Berman's *Aguila o sol*, the Man with Two Heads. This character (these characters) offer(s) two opposite, but equally valid, perspectives to Moctezuma of the course to be followed after the arrival of the new visitors:

> *Una Cabeza.* Como sea, hay que matarlos.
> *Otra Cabeza.* ¿Y si reviven furiosos?
> *Una Cabeza.* ¿Y si los bienvenimos y eran menos que nosotros?
> *Otra Cabeza.* ¿Y si los matamos y nos traían un sol más blanco?
> *Una Cabeza.* ¿Y si nos matan y no traían más que cacahuates?

> [*One Head.* They should be killed, one way or another.
> *Other Head.* And if they come back to life furious?
> *One Head.* And if we welcome them and they were below us?
> *Other Head.* And if we kill them and they were bringing us a whiter sun?
> *One Head.* And if they kill us and they were bringing nothing but peanuts?]

> (*AS*, 233–34)

Another important example of the unitary and at the same time diverse character of historical (and theatrical) reality is dramatized in the disputes among indigenous groups. The image of the Tlaxcaltecs supporting the invaders in their fight against Moctezuma destroys the false and reductionist vision of homogeneity imposed on the precolumbian people who occupied Mesoamerica.

Returning to the intertextual level, it appears to be neither accidental nor surprising that Berman's drama is linked with historical and historiographic texts such as *La visión de los vencidos,* the sixteenth-century *Códice Florentino,* the *Lienzo de Tlaxcala,* and with Muñoz Camargo's *Historia de Tlaxcala* (see "PC," 2). But the link between Berman's drama and Paz's poetic prose text *¿Aguila o sol?* (1950), whose central preoccupation is the Word, is somewhat more enigmatic:

> Recorrí dos calles más, tiritando, cuando de pronto sentí—no, no sentí: pasó, rauda, la Palabra. Lo inesperado del encuentro me paralizó por un segundo, que fue suficiente para darle tiempo de volver a la noche. Repuesto, alcancé a cogerla por las puntas del pelo flotante. Tiré desesperadamente de esas hebras que se alargaban hacia el infinito, hilos de telégrafo que se alejan irremediablemente con un paisaje entrevisto, nota que sube, se adelgaza, se estira, se estira. . . . Me quedé solo en mitad de la calle, con una pluma roja entre las manos amoratadas.

> [I walked two blocks more, shivering, when suddenly I felt—no, I didn't feel: it passed, quickly: the Word. The unexpectedness of the meeting paralyzed me for a second, enough to give it time to return to the night. Recovered, I chased and grabbed it by the tips of its floating hair. I pulled desperately and those hairs that stretch toward the infinite, telegraph wires that move out with a landscape glimpsed, sign that rises, tapers off, stretches out, stretches out. . . . I was alone in the middle of the street, with a red feather between my livid hands.] (P/*AS*, 12/13)

In this hybrid text (prose or poem?), Paz—using, among other things, *jitanjáforas*—explores and delights in the links and disparities between signifier and signified, between the literal and the metaphorical, among the multiple meanings of words.[13] But, above all, Paz's text metaphorizes the relationship that language in general, and words in particular, establish with the speaker, with the person who creates words and whose existence depends on them. In a parallel way, Berman's drama focuses on the linguistic aspect by making recourse not only to comic and vulgar language, but also to language that is meaningless, flawed or reminiscent of Cantinflas ("cantinfladas"), which is embodied chiefly in the discourse of Cortés. About the ambiguous character of verbal construction, Cypess remarks: "Berman focuses directly on the instability of the linguistic signs as a way to demonstrate a lack of reliance on and a mistrust of all verbal constructs, historical documents, and the patriarchal tradition. . . . Berman attacks the tightly bound paradigms of traditional discourse in her portrayal of the principal players in the encounter" ("CC," 500).

In Berman's play, there are two important instances that showcase the gap between speaker and discourse, and between the literal and the symbolic. These are the conversation between the Third Wise Man and the Drunk, and the baptism that Ixtlixuchitl tries to impose on his family. In the first case, the traditional expectation with respect to a drunkard's discourse is that it will be characterized by non-sense, incoherence, and fragmentation. But, ironically, it is the Drunk who most keenly and clearly denounces the inconsistencies of Moctezuma and the inevitable triumph of the invaders (AS, 247–48). In the second example, one sees the grotesque disparity between the baptismal message as a symbol of life and salvation, and the scene in which Yocotzin, who dies by her son's hand, is brought by him before the priest to be baptized (AS, 251–52). Ironically, Ixtlixuchitl distorts the symbolic meaning of renewal through water by burning his mother's house, in which she dies as a result of the fire. Applying "water" by means of "fire" and killing a mother to "save" her represent gross contradictions at the physical as well as the symbolic level. For this reason, one recognizes immediately that neither the old nor the new Christians manage to integrate the literal dimension with the figurative, in which baptism is the giver of life and not an instrument of death. But the most important characterization and impeachment of verbal and theatrical communication is dramatized in the incoherent and absurd speeches of Cortés. For example, the conquistador's response to his first encounter with Moctezuma's emissaries characterizes the gap between verbal expressions and their meaning.

> Cortés. ¿Gato por liebre, sucios negros trajinantes? Mas cus-cus ¿io?: ¿nieve de orozuz.
> Los enviados han escuchado confundidos el idioma "extanjero" de Cortés. Malinche traduce:
> Malinche. Dice Cortés: ¿no es una emboscada?

> [Cat for a hare, you dirty black traffickers? But 'fraid ¿me-o? Licorice ice.[14]
> The emissaries are confused on hearing Cortés's "foreign" language. Malinche translates:
> Malinche. Cortés says: isn't it an ambush?]

(AS, 234)

Or, later on, when the baptisms of the Tlazcaltecs (especially that of Ixtlixuchitl) take place and the history of Judeo-Christian cosmogony is narrated, Cortés says:

> *Cortés.* Espíritu Santus pater de Cristus. Cristus pater de Carlus Quintus. Carlus Quintus pater di Cortés. Y Cortés, io, pater di todus estus nacus, ¡ostia!

> [*Cortés.* Espíritu Santus pater de Cristus. Cristus pater de Carlus Quintus. Carlus Quintus pater di Cortés. Y Cortés, io, pater di todus estus nacus, dammit!]

$$(AS, 251)^{15}$$

As Cypess points out, Cortés speaks broken Spanish throughout the work, a bastard version of Castillian that includes expressions in other languages and even words that originate at times posterior to the history of the Conquest ("CC," 501). She points out as well the political angle of this important linguistic transgression in *Aguila o sol* by linking Cortés's use of foreign and anachronistic terms with the imperialistic role that a number of countries, such as France, Italy, Germany, and the United States, played (and continue to play) in the history of Mexico at the political, economic, and cultural level ("CC," 501). Along with this political dimension, Cypess points out how this linguistic distortion allows La Malinche to establish a close relationship with the audience, which needs her to understand Cortés's nonsense: "By means of the linguistic game, moreover, Berman encourages audience identification with the conquered Indians and not with the conquerors" ("CC," 501). Finally, though, what I wish to emphasize about the linguistic aspect is the intertextual dialogue between Berman's play and homonymous texts in which verbal histrionics turn out to be a central element. Already mentioned is the fact that in Paz's *¿Aguila o sol?* the main character is the Word, which the Mexican author not only personifies but plays with:

> Te desfondo a fondo, te desfundo de tu fundamento. Traquetea tráquea aquea. El carrascaloso se rasca la costra de caspa. Doña campamocha se atasca, tarasca. El sinuoso, el silbante babeante, al pozo con el gozo. Al pozo de ceniza. El erizo se irisa, se eriza, se riza de risa. Sopa de sapos, cepo de pedos, todos a una, bola de sílabas de estropajo, bola de gargajo, bola de vísceras de sílabas sibilas, badajo, sordo badajo. Jadeo, penduleo desguaniguilado, jadeo.

> [I soundly unground you, I unfound your foundation. Squeak creak Greek. The he-man twitches with itches of dandruff. Lady Rotrock

bitches and snaps. The curly girl, the dribbling sibling in the eddy so heady. In the eddy of ash. The thistle whistles, bristles, buckles with chuckles. Broth of moths, chart of farts, all together, ball of syllables of waste matters, ball of snot splatter, ball of the viscera of syllable sybils, chatter deaf chatter. I flap, I swing smashdunguided, I flap.]
(P/AS, 14/15)

On hearing Cortés's speeches and this selection from Paz, how can one not think immediately of the wordplay of the famous Mexican comedian Mario Moreno, alias Cantinflas? How can one not be reminded of the torrent of words, the interminable anacoluthons and malapropisms that characterize his speech, and that have made him world famous?[16] Nor is it an accident that the title of one of Cantinflas's films is precisely, as Hugo Argüelles reminds us, *Aguila o sol* (see note 12, below).

What I am trying to show, in the end, is how Berman employs a certain intertextual dialogue, characterized and defined by the use and abuse of verbal construction, to impart to her work a significant dose of self-reflexiveness, in which the vehicle of communication constructs an ironic and irreverent vision of history and at the same time dismantles that vision by means of a language whose sense resides in nonsense. Paz's *jitanjáforas*, Cantinflas's wordplay and anacoluthons, and the malapropisms that Berman puts into the mouth of Cortés and that are translated by La Malinche, draw our attention to these linguistic games which, in turn, underline the anti-institutional and antitraditional nature of verbal communication. We see, then, how the use and abuse of theatrical language and of linguistic codes is manifested in their double function as objects for, and of, attack. Paz recreates this world replete with contradictions most skillfully:

Su amor por la vida obliga a desertar la vida; su amor al lenguaje lleva al desprecio de las palabras; su amor al juego conduce a pisotear las reglas, a inventar otras, a jugarse la vida en una palabra.... Abstraído en una meditación—que consiste en ser una meditación sobre la inutilidad de la meditaciones, una contemplación en la que el que contempla es contemplado por lo que contempla y ambos por la Contemplación, hasta que los tres son uno—se rompen los lazos con el mundo, la razón y el lenguaje.

[This love of life requires that we desert life; this love of language makes us scorn the words; this love of games moves us to trample on the rules, to invent others, to gamble life on a word.... Secluded in meditation that is a meditation on the uselessness of meditations, a

contemplation in which he who contemplates is also being contem-
plated, by that which he is contemplating, and both in turn by contemplation, until the three are one, and the links with life, reason, and
language are broken.]

(P/AS, 14, 16/15, 17)

In *Aguila o sol,* as in many of Berman's plays, she frequently
exalts dismantling, fragmentation, evasiveness, the un-fixed, the
categorical evasion of the categorical, and the paradoxical nature
of theatrical and linguistic construction.[17] For this reason, it has
been pertinent to examine Berman's play here in the light of those
vast and sometimes contradictory reflections on the culture of
postmodernism that emphasize paradox itself. According to
Linda Hutcheon, the paradoxical and contradictory nature of
postmodernism is the reason that the most penetrating of cultural
critics and scholars have felt called to investigate the topic: "What
their debates have shown is that the postmodern is, if it is anything, a problemizing force in our culture today: it raises questions about (or renders problematic) the common-sensical and
the 'natural.' But it never offers answers that are anything but
provisional and contextually determined (and limited)" (*P*, xi). But
what is even more enlightening is the emphasis that postmodern
discourse places on incorporating (and delighting in) all that
which questions or subverts (see *P*, 3). Parody, then "is a perfect
postmodern form, in some senses, for it paradoxically both incorporates and challenges that which it parodies" (*P*, 11).

Examining *Aguila o sol* from a linguistic perspective in which
verbal transgression is converted into the symbol of theatrical
transgression, and vice versa, and recognizing at the same time
the persistent dismantling of the values and conventions that these
two languages attempt to define, we come up against the paradoxical characterization of an art that is categorical about its anti-
categorical and anti-authoritarian postures. We see in *Aguila o sol*
the Mexican dramatist's attempt to decipher what results or arises
when rupture is dramatized by means of transgression. To break
with transgression—which in the last analysis represents a going
beyond the modern which feeds on crisis—would appear to be a
double negation. But in *Aguila o sol* this double negation is what
formulates its simultaneous and plural reality. The Conquest, according to Berman, is theatre and its reverse; it is a schema whose
apparent coherence recreates an absurd and unintelligible drama
and whose principal communicative structure—theatre—is an il-
logical and incoherent language. Theatre, then, turns out to be

as deceptive and manipulative as historiography has been, and the fact that Berman turns to a disparaged genre such as farce and other forms of popular theatre—to street theatre and the circus tent—becomes a way of questioning traditional, institutional, and even ideological theatre.[18] Thus, from the point of view of *Aguila o sol,* the dramatization of the Conquest—that is, its staging—is an oxymoron, a contradiction in terms; a gesture both self-generating and self-destructive, it is both cosmic and comic.

Aguila o sol emphasizes in this way the fragmented and parodical relationship that the play establishes with the documents on which it is based, with the instability of the interior and exterior world of the conquistadors and the conquered, and with the verbal and dramatic codes that Berman constructs and dismantles on stage. Finally, the dramatization of the crisis of narrative history permits Berman to question, or simply assume an attitude of incredulity, toward the possibility of substituting one version for another, casting aside one ideological discourse for another. The "unity," the "identity," the "cohesiveness" of a people, and the attempt to achieve cultural, linguistic, and theatrical definition, are submitted in *Aguila o sol* to severe scrutiny and parodization. Berman's capacity for transgressing historical and theatrical discourse beyond what has already been transgressed by the discourse of modernity, for categorically rejecting the categorical, and for dramatizing linguistic complexity by means of communicative as well as thematic fragmentation, can be connected more explicitly to the postmodern nature of art. *Aguila o sol* not only perpetrates a questioning of history, of the individual personality, of the relationship of language to its referents, and of the relationship of texts to other texts (see *P,* xiii), it also inquires into the very linguistic, ideological, philosophical, and aesthetic instruments that are used to ask the questions.

It is precisely in the context of postmodernism that it becomes pertinent to turn to the comments of Roberto González Echevarría. In his lucid text *La ruta de Severo Sarduy,* he points out one of the most important contributions (and transgressions) made by the Cuban writer's work to the discussion of postmodern art. His comments might very well be applied to Berman's play: "Sarduy's work hangs over Spanish American literature like a question mark, because it threatens not only traditional literary ideology, which all modern works inevitably attack, but also the points of reference from which modern works attack that tradition."[19] In a parallel way, it can be said that *Aguila o sol* not only attacks those dramatic texts—written principally by men—that seem to question traditional literary and political ideologies about Mexican history, it also attacks the verbal, dramatic, and theoretical constructions that serve to support the attack on tradition.

Notes

My immense gratitude to my dear friend and colleague from Michigan State University, Patricia Lunn, for translating this essay into English.

1. Some of the better-known works that make use of the dramatization of important events in Mexican history are Rodolfo Usigli's *Corona de sombra* (1943) and *Corona de fuego* (1960); Celestino Gorostiza's *La Malinche* (1958); Salvador Novo's *Cuauhtémoc* (1962); Sergio Magaña's *Cortés y La Malinche* (or *Los argonautas*, 1967); Carlos Fuentes's *Todos los gatos son pardos* (1970); Vicente Leñero's *El juicio* (1971) and *Martirio de Morelos* (1981); and Emilio Carballido's *Almanaque de Juárez* (1972). In implicit reference to the works of some of these dramatists, Sandra Messinger Cypess points out in "From Colonial Constructs to Feminist Figures: Re/visions by Mexican Women Dramatists," *Theatre Journal* 41, no. 4 (1989) that: "The contemporary use of theatrical form to present an ideological critique of culture continues that tradition of the missionaries in a provocative new way. A number of plays recreate on stage aspects of the colonial past that offer a contemporary interpretation of the colonial situation; that is, they constitute a re-reading that in the re-enactment of the colonial situation, questions the validity of the received history" (494). Hereafter "CC," cited in the text.

2. At the end of Kirsten Nigro's "Rhetoric and History in Three Mexican Plays," *Latin American Theatre Review* 21, no. 1 (1987): 6, she emphasizes the link between the three pieces she examines and the historical context from which they emerge, i.e., Mexico in the 1950s and 1960s: "Thus the three plays studied here are not only a lesson in the past, but also in the present that produced them. . . . For as *La Malinche*, *Cuauhtémoc* and *Corona de fuego* demonstrate, history's theatrical offshoots are complex discourses that go well beyond the innocent, objective fact to influence . . . their public into a particular way of seeing the here and now through a far from transparent rendering of what once was" (72). Hereafter "RH," cited in the text.

3. See Jacqueline Bixler, "Re-casting the Past: The Dramatic Debunking of Mexico's 'Official' History," *Revista Hispánica Moderna* 42, no. 2 (1989): 163. Hereafter "R," cited in the text.

4. Cypess studies Rosario Castellano's *El eterno femenino* and Berman's *Aguila o sol* as part of an examination of the feminist perspective in the construction and revision of the colonial past. For her part, Bixler demonstrates how Jorge Ibargüengoitia's *El atentado*, Wilfredo López's *Yo soy Juárez*, and Vicente Leñero's *Martirio de Morelos* question the veracity and authority of official Mexican history through the reformulation of certain episodes and the casting of certain "heroes" in an unfavorable light ("Re-casting," 163). Even when both theatre and historiography tend to elevate the quotidian or the common, Bixler points out that: "these playwrights seek the opposite effect, using satire and irony to demagnify and deflate the myths that have petrified along with the paradoxically named Partido Revolucionario Institucional" (ibid., 164).

5. Cypess recognizes the important contribution of contemporary male dramatists, but recognizes as well the position of power from which they hand down their criticism of official history: "Their work was important in stimulating the scrutiny of the official historical record not as fact but as stereotyped accounts or false representations of the

historical reality. Thus, at the same time their plays explore national themes they are motivated by an underlying philosophical inquisition into the complex relationship between reality and fiction, between history and truth, and between history and literature. Once the production of discourse related to 'history' is interrogated, *an analysis of the producers themselves can be pursued* [emphasis added]. This approach yields the realization that there has been indeed a *fellow*ship of discourse and those who have been excluded are the people marginalized from the power center because of class, race, and gender. Since women in Mexico, as in other countries, have not participated in the formation of discourse until recently, their perspectives have not formed part of the 'official history' (it has indeed been History and not Herstory)" ("Colonial Constructs," 494–95). In another of Cypess's essays, "Dramaturgia femenina y transposición histórica," *Alba de América* 7, nos. 12–13 (1989), she examines how Elena Garro, Rosario Castellanos, and Sabina Berman become part of the Mexican cultural revisionist enterprise which questions the validity of the sacred myths of this society: "It is important that they have entered as women into the discursive site that previously silenced the feminine version of the world and relegated women's works to a secondary place. The attack on official history seen in these works [*Felipe Angeles, El eterno femenino,* and *Aguila o sol*] also helps to demystify the official concept of 'the feminine' in the social and aesthetic realms" (301).

6. Jorge Luis Borges, "El Zahir," in *El Aleph* (Buenos Aires: Emecé, 1957), 112. Hereafter "Z," cited in the text. Using the image of the coin suspended in the air, one can suggest the possible answer that Berman's text might give to the questions that, according to Susan Rubin Suleiman in "Feminism and Postmodernism: A Question of Politics," in *Zeitgeist in Babel: The Postmodernist Controversy,* ed. Ingerborg Hoestery (Bloomington: Indiana University Press, 1991), constantly come up about the political role of postmodern feminist art. These questions reveal the tension between the politicization of art and its ironic dimension, which tends to distance the work from its political intentions: "[C]an art which claims an oppositional edge take the risk of entering a museum? Can it afford to be negative and individualistic, rather than offering a positive, collective 'alternative vision' of 'how things might be different'" (121; Suleiman cites Martha Rosler, "Notes on Quotes").

7. See Sabina Berman, *Aguila o sol,* in *Teatro de Sabina Berman* (Mexico: Editores Mexicanos Unidos, 1985), 240. Hereafter *AS,* cited in the text. All textual references are from this edition. It should be remembered that the work itself emphasizes the internal struggles between the Cholultecs and the Tlaxcaltecs which result in the massacre at Cholula (245–47).

8. Linda Hutcheon, *A Poetics of Postmodernism: History, Theory, Fiction* (New York: Routledge, 1988), 5. Hereafter *P,* cited in the text. It is not surprising that the most characteristic qualities that Suleiman identifies for describing the postmodern style should be pertinent to the analysis and characterization of Berman's *Aguila o sol:* "the appropriation, misappropriation, montage, collage, hybridization, and general mixing up of visual and verbal texts and discourses, for all periods of the past as well as from the multiple social and linguistic fields of the present" ("Feminism," 118). But, above all, Suleiman argues that the central question that arises with respect to the postmodern debate is whether the meaning and effects produced by this style are political, or whether they constitute nothing more than a parody without meaning or importance: "Does this style have a critical political meaning or effect, or is it—in Fredric Jameson's words—merely 'blank parody,' a 'neutral practice' devoid of any critical impulse or historical consciousness?" (ibid.). If one had to examine closely the pertinence of this question for Berman's drama, one would have to focus instead on the relationship between feminism and postmodernism that Suleiman herself points out, and even see how Berman parodies this alliance: "[F]eminism brings to postmodernism the political guarantee postmodernism needs in order to feel respectable as an avant-garde practice. Postmodernism, in turn,

brings feminism into a certain kind of 'high theoretical' discourse on the frontiers of culture, traditionally an exclusively male domain" (ibid., 116).

9. See Keir Elam, "Theatrical Communication: Codes, Systems and the Performance Text," in *The Semiotics of Theatre and Drama* (New York: Methuen, 1980), 32–97.

10. See Jeanne Gillespie, "Political Commentary and the Conquest in Sabina Berman's Drama *Aguila o sol.*" Paper presented at the thirteenth annual Cincinnati Conference on Romance Languages and Literatures, May 1993. Hereafter "PC," cited in the text. See also Sandra Cypess, "Ethnic Identity in the Plays of Sabina Berman," in *Tradition and Innovation: Reflections on Latin American Jewish Writing,* ed. Robert Di Antonio and Nora Glickman (New York: State University of New York Press, 1993). Although Cypess concentrates in this insightful study on the examination of *Herejía* from the point of view of Mexico's religious history with regard to the Jews, she also sees in *Aguila o sol* the exploration of the formation of national identity and ethnicity, "especially the idea of the definition of the self within a multicultural nation" (165): "*Herejía,* like *Aguila o sol,* exposes the lie inherent in the concept that Mexican cultural identity is a single, monotone hegemonic voice" (176–77).

11. Cypess points out: "The audience/reader's expectation is that Cortés would speak in a language that would be understood by the audience, since a concomitant feature of colonialism is the imposition of the language of the dominant culture on the colonized peoples. It is not Cortés who is intelligible to the audience, but the Indians" ("Colonial Constructs," 501). For her part, Gillespie emphasizes the fact that these senseless speeches of Cortés are quite different from the version of the encounter offered by the *Códice Florentino*—a sixteenth-century text commissioned by the Franciscan friar Bernardino de Sahagún and written in Nahuatl—in which Cortés reveals his aptitude for communication: "Since the treatment of Cortés represents the most radical departure from the texts upon which Berman has based this dramatization, an analysis of the language and images with which Berman describes the captain provides further insight into the dramatist's attack on 'historical consciousness.' Although Cortés babbles until the face to face meeting with Moctezuma, some of the utterances may be decoded by the actions the captain performs and by the translation of Malinche" ("Political Commentary," 5–6).

12. It is necessary to mention the poetic prose text written by Octavio Paz between 1949 and 1950 entitled ¿*Aguila o sol?* See ¿*Aguila o sol?/Eagle or Sun?* Bilingual edition, trans. Eliot Weinberger (New York: October House, 1970). Hereafter P/AS, cited in the text; page numbers are carried for both the Spanish and English versions. The title, as has been pointed out, differs from Berman's in the presence of question marks. Other aspects of this text by Paz which will permit a close link to be established between it and Berman's text will be examined below. For the time being, I simply suggest the intertextual character of Berman's drama and the "coincidence" of the title with other Mexican artistic expressions. For example, in Hugo Argüelles's brief essay "Crónica como prólogo para otra crónica," in *Teatro de Sabina Berman,* 214, he alludes to a Cantinflas film entitled *Aguila o sol,* and from other sources I have come across the 1923 novel *Aguila o sol* by the Mexican Heriberto Frías.

13. The term *jitanjáfora* was invented by Alfonso Reyes as a result of his reading of the collection of poetry by the Cuban Mariano Brull, *Poemas en menguante (1928).* See Alfonso Reyes, "Las jitanjáforas," in *La experiencia literaria,* 3d ed. (Buenos Aires: Losada, 1969), 182–226. The term, as defined by Fernando Lázaro Carreter in *Diccionario de términos filológicos,* 3d ed. (Madrid: Gredos, 1977), is meant to "designate words, metaphors, onomatopoeias, interjections, rhymes, etc., which have no meaning, but which constitute a powerful stimulus for the imagination" (252).

14. I follow here Sandra Cypess's translation of this sentence as found in "Colonial Constructs," 501.

15. With reference to this scene, Gillespie penetratingly points out: "While Malinche narrates the story of the original sin and then the Immaculate Conception with a puppet show, Cortés assumes the role of 'father/padrino/tocayo' affirming his 'lineage'. . . . The combination of the Immaculate Conception story and Cortés's convoluted self-image as a 'Holy Father,' when viewed in the context of the sexual subtext of the drama, adds an incestuous element to the Spaniard's activities" ("Political Commentary," 9).

16. Lázaro Carreter defines anacoluthon as the "abandon of the syntactic construction required in one context to adopt another more in line with what the speaker is thinking at that moment, forgetting grammatical coherence (*Diccionario*, 41), and malapropism "applies to the deformation and poor usage of foreign words" (*Diccionario*, 270).

17. I have examined Berman's obsession with escaping from the obvious, the fixed, the predictable, in another of her works, *El suplicio del placer* (1978). I refer the reader to my article "(In)Decency and (Dis)Pleasure: Women and Farce in Sabina Berman's *El suplicio del placer*," which will form part of my forthcoming book *Farce and Falseness in Spanish American Theatre*.

18. In his brief piece on *Aguila o sol*, Argüelles points out that Berman's work "recalls in its tone and its treatment much of the best of the almost extinct tradition of the *Mexican circus tent*, precisely . . . when it engages in that kind of poking fun at our unassuageable sorrows (which are more than ancestral, as is that of the Conquest)" ("Crónica," 215, emphasis added). According to John B. Nomland, in his *Teatro mexicano contemporáneo (1900–1950),* trans. Paloma Borostiza de Zozaya and Luis Reyes de la Maza (Mexico: Instituto Nacional de Bellas Artes, 1967), the rise of the circus tent goes back to the end of the Mexican Revolution. Economic collapse and the difficulty of moving from one part of a city to another inspired the theatrical impresarios to move their variety companies into portable tents: "the initial idea was . . . to put up a tent on bare ground . . . install a wooden platform and build seats from boards" (171). With respect to the audiences and the content of the shows, Nomland adds: "It should be taken into consideration that the diversion offered in the tents is directed to the working class, ignorant of the subtleties of dramatic art, but quite willing to laugh and applaud the dancers, the acrobats, the husky singers and the quick-witted comedians." "Among the different kinds of works represented in the tent are pantomimes, monologues, dialogues, short sketches, comic pieces or farces just one act long, scenes from *zarzuelas* and short operas and theatrical works" (172, 173).

19. Roberto González Echevarría, *La ruta de Severo Sarduy* (Hanover, N.H.: Ediciones del Norte, 1987), iii.

Myth and Metatheatre: Magaña's Malinche and Medea

Sandra Messinger Cypess
University of Maryland

I N *El perfil del hombre y la cultura en México,* Samuel Ramos wrote that Mexicans do not know their own history. Yet, at the same time, other historians have suggested that Mexicans are obsessed with history.[1] Certainly, the number of plays that deal with historical topics attests to the fascination of Mexican writers with the past and with an investigation of the past as a means to understand the present. The bibliography relating to such topics is vast, the uses of the historical and dramatic elements multiple. My purpose in this essay is not to offer a general bibliographic review or to present general statements but to focus on one key historical event that has been mythicized in Mexican culture, the Conquest, and to explore how one dramatist links the Conquest and its key figures to another, unexpected mythic event, that of the Medea-Jason story. I refer to Sergio Magaña and *Los argonautas,* a play first produced in 1967 and then renamed *Cortés y La Malinche* for subsequent productions and publication. I shall explore the two extratextual referents upon which Magaña builds his play—the Medea myth and the Conquest—and then suggest some of the implications of his thematic and technical choices.

Magaña has not been one of the Mexican playwrights whose work is read routinely, or criticized in any regular way, yet most of his plays reflect a keen sense of theatricality, an original approach to common themes, and a mordant sense of humor that should please audiences and critical readers. Magaña also experimented with dramatic forms, exploring metatheatrical techniques that have been studied with regularity in writers from Rodolfo Usigli to Sabina Berman. In addition, like "el maestro" Usigli or his friend Emilio Carballido, Magaña has turned his attention to themes involving Mexican history, adding to the Mexican preoccupation with history in *Moctezuma II,* which first appeared in 1953, and *Cortés y La Malinche.* In grounding his retelling of the Conquest within the paradigm of the Medea myth, Magaña not only suggests a common idea in Mexican culture, that history repeats itself, but he also acknowledges the idea that history is affected in its retelling by the ideology of the narrator. As Magaña comments in the epigraph to the playscript, "de la historia, conjunto de datos falsos, hacemos una obra de arte, que es la única verdad" [from history, a union of false data, we make a work of art, which is the only truth].[2] We need to ask, therefore, why Magaña, unlike the majority of narrators of the Conquest, has chosen the Medea paradigm, and what are the "truths" he wishes to impart to his audience.

Magaña seems to indicate by his use of a mythic subtext that "la historia siempre es la misma" [history always is the same] (*CM,* 150), as his character Bernal Díaz so states in his remarks to the audience at the play's inception. While history may repeat, what *does not* is the manner of narrativization of the events. The contrast between Magaña's manipulation of historical elements and that of his compatriots brings out clearly their differing ideologies. Magaña's view is the most satiric and cynical of the plays of the sixties, and in his irreverence toward the Conquest and its participants anticipates both Rosario Castellanos in *El eterno femenino* (1975) and Sabina Berman's tone in *Aguila o sol* (Eagle or sun, 1984).[3]

Before discussing the particular implications of the Medea myth, it is useful to review the sociohistorical and aesthetic context in which Magaña was working when he wrote the play. Celestino Gorostiza, Salvador Novo, and Usigli had already produced their dramatic versions of the Conquest. Despite the different styles and techniques, and the fact that they questioned official history or popular culture, they configured their renditions of the Conquest within a christianized vocabulary, using the Adam and Eve story as the paradigm within which to explain motivations and outcomes.

Gorostiza, for example, in *La Malinche o la leña está verde* (La Malinche or the firewood is green, 1958) undertakes the difficult task of vindicating La Malinche of her role as traitor and Cortés as vagabond, an assignment that may remind us of Usigli's enterprise in *Corona de sombra* (Crown of shadows) with regard to another infamous couple, Maximilano and Carlota. Both dramatists attempt to provide a context of explanation for unpopular historical figures. In Gorostiza's version, he romanticizes both Malinche and Cortés, and presents the Conquest as an acceptable event because it produced the mestizo nation. In other words, the focus of action centers on the production of the child, so that his play suggests that the coupling of the Indian Malinche and the Spaniard Cortés was destined to occur in order to bring about the mestizo nation. Malinche is transformed into the westernized, christianized doña Marina within the pattern provided by Bernal Díaz de Castillo in his chronicle, as I have shown in *La Malinche in Mexican Literature*. When Usigli focuses on the Conquest in *Corona de fuego* (Crown of fire, 1961) he also glorifies *mestizaje,* but instead of centering his exploration of events on the couple, he uses the story of Cuauhtémoc and his death at the hands of Cortés, and somehow makes of the Indian leader a westernized, christianized symbol of Mexican national identity. Cuauhtémoc is shown to be the victim of Indian disloyalty as much as Spanish treachery, being betrayed by Mexicaltzinco so that Cortés has the evidence necessary to execute him. La Malinche is thus not the only figure who "sells out" to the foreigners. In the scene in which Cuauhtémoc is to be hanged, the stage directions require that the image of a cross be projected onto the ceiba tree. Usigli introduces Christian symbolism to suggest that Cuauhtémoc is sacrificing himself in order to bring about the glorious "nación mexicana":

> Y yo, que pierdo todas las batallas,
> sé que habrá de surgir en el futuro,
> la nación mexicana por que muero . . .

> [and I, who have lost all the battles,
> know that there will arise in the future,
> the Mexican nation for whom I die . . .][4]

While Usigli stresses the epic nature of the Conquest by his choice of a Greek classical format, creating what Kirsten Nigro rightly called a "pseudo-Greek tragedy" for the "elevated language, the use of verse, choric commentary and debate, the ponderous rhythm,"[5] his theme is very unclassical, stressing as it does that *mestizaje* was made possible through Cuauhtémoc's Christian-like sacrifice of self.

When Novo presents his *Cuauhtémoc* the following year, elements of the Greek classical stage techniques are visible in his use of masks for all his characters, but he also incorporates elements of epic theatre in the use of a narrator. Novo indicates in the stage directions that the narrator be an Indian who also takes on the role of Cuauhtémoc in the interior play. The use of the metatheatrical device of a play within a play does not lead to a satiric vision, as it will in Magaña's play, but it does suggest that the contemporary audience should apply the lessons of the Conquest to the contemporary moment. The inability of the indigenous people to withstand the Spanish invasion becomes here not so much a destined event, but a failure of the Indian nation to unite as a democratic unit and fight a common enemy. Cuauhtémoc's vision of a unified, democratic nation is his gift to the future, making of him a true father of the Mexican people, indigenous or mestizo. While ethnicity is also at issue here, more important is the political vision formed by Novo and given to the narrator-Cuauhtémoc to express:

> Cuauhtémoc no ha muerto. Sé que está en mí; que vivirá siempre; en mí y en mis hijos—y en todos los que vengan despúes—a nacer en la tierra de México—formados con los huesos de nuestros muertos—nutridos como el sol con la sangre de nuestros corazones.

> [Cuauhtémoc has not died. I know that he is in me; that he will live forever, in me and in my children—and in all who follow—who will be born in the land of Mexico—formed with the bones of our dead—nourished like the sun with the blood of our hearts.][6]

Whereas Usigli used Christian symbols, Novo invokes the Aztec religious symbols of "the blood of our hearts" in accordance with his stress of the indigenous legacy of Mexico.[7] His Cuauhtémoc is a forward-looking prince of a man, with a modern political sensibility, as Nigro observes, yet he reiterates the popular stereotypes regarding Malinche and Cortés and makes Cuauhtémoc "and not Cortés's mestizo son the emblem of what Mexico was to become."[8]

When Magaña undertakes a revision of the Conquest, all the familiar characters are present, but he adds his own special elements so that his is not a mere rehashing, but a sort of contestation to the previous plays referred to above as well as to the historical record itself. Magaña develops further the epic theatrical devices of Novo and also pays tribute to the Greek theatrical tradition—not like Usigli, who took the form, but by recasting his version of the story as a form of a Greek classical myth, that of Medea and Jason. Our questions concerning Magaña's purpose regarding his appropriation of the historical record may be answered by first reviewing the nature of the Medea myth and how Magaña links it to the key event in Mexican history.

The story of Medea was very popular in classical times and the Euripidean play has inspired many others, including Seneca, Jean Anouilh, Robinson Jeffers, and José Triana *(Medea en el espejo)*. The broad outline of the plot, as given to us by Euripides, focuses on Medea and the themes of love, exile, betrayal, and death; Jason is clearly the villain, an ungrateful opportunist who betrays the woman who gave up everything for his love. According to the myth, Jason had come to Colchis to secure the Golden Fleece and restore it to Hellas. Jason received the assistance of the gods in his task when Aphrodite bribed her son Eros to use his arrows to pierce the heart of Medea, daughter of the King of Colchis and wise in the ways of magic and sorcery. Unable to resist Eros, she could not help but fall in love with Jason, despite her strong feelings of loyalty to her father. After Jason made a sacred oath to marry her, Medea told Jason how to fulfill the tasks her father had set for him, much as Malinche is said to have helped Cortés in understanding how to deal with the Indians. In some versions, Medea goes so far as to harm both her father and her brother before fleeing with Jason; her family represents the Indian peoples whom Malinche abandons in favor of helping the Spaniards. Despite her proven loyalty to Jason, he subsequently abandons her in a strange land when he decides to marry a younger woman, the daughter of King Creon of Corinth. Medea had sacrificed her own national and familial loyalties for his sake, and she plots her revenge for Jason's perfidy by killing his new bride. Medea goes even further in the Euripidean version by killing the children she bore Jason, her final vengeance for her spouse's own treachery.[9] The transformation of her intense love into fierce hate with the attendant destruction of those dearest to her reflect the dark, deep-lying aspects of unrestrained love and immoderate scorn. Medea, however, appears a tragic heroine in the way she sacrifices all for love, but Jason is a treacherous figure in that he is motivated by greed and self-fulfillment.

The relationship between the Medea myth and the Conquest had already been suggested once by Jesús Sotelo Inclán in his play *Malintzin (Medea americana),* published in 1957. That play is not dramatically effective, although it is important to note that Sotelo Inclán seems to be among the first to suggest that Malinche's behavior follows the Medea paradigm. Using a pseudo-epic poetic form, he covers the life of Malinche until 1524, and tries to vindicate her, too, as the mother of the mestizo nation. She is a Medea figure for Sotelo Inclán in the way she abandons her fatherland out of love for the stranger, only to be abandoned in turn. At one point, Malintzin says that she has saved Indian blood by having a child with Cortés,[10] but as her hatred for Cortés grows, she also admits to be willing to kill her child if Cortés would try to take him from her.[11] Magaña, in contrast, does not elaborate on the infanticide issue, although he does continue the motif of tying Malinche's continued loyalty to Cortés on the basis of the child she bears him.[12]

Magaña's play is far more interesting and entertaining than Sotelo Inclán's, especially in its use of humor and satire. Also, he prefers to focus on the economic and political issues implicit in Jason's desire for the Golden Fleece. He presents the connections between the Medea-Jason legend and the Malinche-Cortés relationship from the onset, so that dropping the title *Los argonautas* does not obscure the subtext. It is essential to review carefully the opening stage business since it is precisely then that Magaña announces to his audience the changes he will be making in the established tradition regarding the (re)telling of the Conquest; he indicates the conventions he follows and the possible liberties he proposes immediately.

An unnamed soldier enters the stage through the closed curtains to address the audience; he is the narrator and will also be one of the characters in the play, as well as the scribe for the events that take place. His appearance indicates that he is a European soldier of the sixteenth century; his first words characterize the story to come as "la historia de una expedición" (*CM*, 149). He then contrasts his perspective with that of his captain, whom he calls "aguerrido," a "veteran" accustomed to war. In the words of the captain, the expedition is a "guerra de conquista," so he acknowledges that the enterprise demands not only acquisitions, but the defeat of the opposing forces.

When the curtain opens fully, a sign is revealed which says "Veracruz 450 km. A Tenochtitlan." Three indigenous warriors watch the invading troops, who file by with food and supplies. The first soldier, who had begun by addressing the audience, continues speaking, indicating the identity of the actors on stage; we learn from him that the Indians, whom he calls variously "hiperbóreos" [hyperboreans] or "anfitriones" [hosts] had given the provisions to the foreigners; these designations are unique and significant, for Bernal resorts here to Greek terms, carefully avoiding "Indian"; according to Greek legend, the hyperboreans lived in a land of sun and warmth, far beyond the north winds, a term loosely applicable to the indigenous peoples the Spaniards met; calling them "anfitriones," or hosts, is clearly caustic in its exaggeration, since their collaboration in providing sustenance to the Spaniards was often brought about through force. The collusion of some of the indigenous peoples in the enterprise is important, however, since there will be other hyperboreans who will not be so willing to provide generous support. The Indians watch as the soldiers continue to take away food, both groups oblivious to the narrator-soldier. He is noticed only when the captain enters. The audience members who are knowledgeable will already have surmised that he is Cortés only from the geographic sign that indicates the east coast of Mexico. The unnamed soldier does not introduce the captain but first gives out the information that his expedition has been likened to another famous journey. His words refer to the myth of Jason and the Argonauts, who went out in search of the Golden Fleece. He asks the audience, "¿Habeis oído algo de eso? No importa. La historia siempre es la misma" [Have you heard anything about that? It doesn't matter. History is always the same] (150). The search for gold that initiated the adventures of the Argonauts will be consistently associated with the behavior of the Spaniards, marking them as greedy opportunists.

After establishing that message, the narrator identifies his function in the enterprise: "Yo me limitaré a manuscribir los acontecimientos en esta libreta y con esta pluma" [I will limit myself to transcribing the events in this book and with this pen] (150). The identity of the narrator is announced when the captain addresses him, so that the first words of the script is the name of the scribe: "¡Soldado Bernal Díaz del Castillo!" Bernal responds by naming his captain, whose identity is obvious to all informed spectators: "Obedezco en seguida, señor capitán Hernán Cortés" [I obey immediately, Sir Captain Hernán Cortés]. The artificiality of his response, that is, giving the whole name of his captain, is further emphasized when Bernal turns once again to the audience to add a comment that sets the tone for the subsequent actions: "No os confieis del estilo ni de la intención. En esta primera parte, sobre todo, el tono es satírico, pero las consecuencias emocionantes" [Don't rely on the style or the intention. In this first part, especially, the tone is satiric, but the consequences thrilling] (150).

The audience learns that the play is a satire and not a record of official history come to life. By focusing on Bernal Díaz as scribe, the playwright introduces the idea that at the same time historical events occur, the narrator of those circumstances may re-cast, re-view, re-do, those events. Bernal's recording of incidents is often interrupted and interfered with by the people in power, whether it is Cortés or Carlos V directly, or Bernal the scribe's own realization of the force of power on official history. One humorous incident shows Magaña's skepticism not only about the truth of the historical record, but about the motivations for the official transcription vis-à-vis the enterprise of the Conquest. Bernal is reading from Cortés's letter to the emperor and then makes his own comments (a synecdoche for the reality of the two texts that were produced historically by the two men):

> Nuestro capitán escribe al emperador que ... "hemos llegado al centro de un gran imperio." (Al público ...) Difiero. Imperio es un concepto europeo. (Moja pluma y se dispone a escribir en la libreta) Corrijo. "Ni esto es un imperio ni la nuestra es una expansión industrial. Es un ejemplo de rapiña contra pueblos mal organizados." (Deja de escribir) Eso es. (Reacciona) ¡No, no! No! Lee esto nuestro capitán Cortés, y adiós Bernal. Tacho. (Pone tache y escribe hablando) "Hemos llegado al corazón mismo de estos pueblos agresivos y idólatras. Nuestro capitán es un gran capitán. ¡Viva el Papa Adriano y viva su Majestad don Carlos!" (Al público) Ligeras concesiones ...

> [Our captain writes to the emperor that ... "we have arrived at the center of a great empire." (To the public ...) I differ. Empire is a European concept. (He wets his pen and begins to write in the book) I make a correction. "This is neither an empire nor is ours an industrial expansion. It is an example of rape against people poorly organized." (He stops writing) That's it. (He reacts) No, no! No! Should our Captain Cortés read this, it's good-bye Bernal. I'll erase it (He crosses it out and writes as he speaks) "We have arrived at the very heart of the empire of these aggressive and idolatrous peoples. Our captain is a great captain. Long live Pope Adriano and long live His Majesty don Carlos! (To the public) Small concessions ...

(CM, 207)

These self-conscious comments of Bernal clearly indicate that Magaña places his work within the discourse of metadrama and metahistory. This discursive category is cogently summarized by Jacqueline Bixler:

> History and drama are both modes of discourse that stem from a dialectical interaction between fiction and reality. Historical drama, the composite of history and theatre, is at once metahistorical and metadramatic in the double vision that it presents the audience. The historical play points simultaneously at historical reality and at the way in which that reality is reenacted, at the dramatic illusion created on the stage as well as at the reality that exists off-stage.[13]

By ignoring the distinctions between reality and fiction, the writer of metatheatre reveals the interrelated nature of the events on stage and off, encouraging the members of the audience to consider the dramatic representation as equally valid as any other (historical) interpretation, or at least to question the representational "truth" of history.

The members of the audience who attend a metatheatrical piece are reminded of their role by the way they are addressed from the stage, as Bernal addresses his audience. They are given the task of watching and judging, a role that is encouraged by Magaña's technique of using spotlights to highlight and isolate the different speakers. This use of spot lighting fulfills a number of dramatic functions. First, Magaña may introduce a number of characters at the same time without the need for temporal or geographic logic; Bernal is thus able to speak directly with Carlos V even though the ruler is still in Spain; Bernal as narrator can also freeze the action and make comments about the characters, emphasizing the metatheatrical nature of the drama and reminding the audience that their role should be one of judge. The spots allow the audience to observe closely each speaker without distractions—distant and removed. The actors appear like specimens of study, under light, while the audience, literally in the darkened house, believe themselves more enlightened than the characters, more knowledgeable. The distancing techniques of epic theatre enable the audience to judge the events and the characters involved while the metatheatrical elements expose not only the artificialities involved in the production of the play, but the artifice of the creation of play, of theater, of history.

Magaña encourages the superiority of his audience vis-à-vis his characters in the way he uses dramatic irony. For example, at one point Cortés must decide what to do with one of the Spaniards who wishes to betray him; he opts to cut off the feet of the traitor, Gonzalo de Umbría, explaining this act with an extratextual reference that the audience will understand, if not the characters: "Siempre he tenido una gran predilección por los pies de la gente" [I've always had a great attraction to the feet of people] (*CM*, 155). This comment projects us to a future event, that will not be part of this dramatic version, when Cortés burns the feet of Cuauhtémoc in order to make him divulge the location of the golden treasure he craves. When the ironic comment is made at this point, the Spaniard's feet are cut off as a lesson to the soldiers who are ready to mutiny as a protest to the lack of gold; once again, the importance of gold and greed as motivating factors in the enterprise of the Conquest relates the actions of Cortés to Jason.

What is also significant here is the way Magaña uses dramatic irony to refer to future actions that his own play will not cover. Aside from enhancing the metatheatrical aspects of the play, this technique emphasizes the themes or personal characteristics that substantiate Magaña's perspective. When Cortés comments that he has a predilection for feet, the members of the audience may laugh (or shudder) as they recall the future event he alludes to, and they may also acknowledge the appropriateness of the text invented by Magaña, the playwright. Another good example of this technique is found in an exchange between Malinche and Cortés. Malinche reminds Cortés of the implications of her fierce love: "Espera, porque si alguna vez te canso y me cambias . . . Te amaré siempre, pero sabré vengarme. Estamos en deuda. No se te olvide" [Wait, because if I should bore you sometime and you exchange me . . . I shall love you always, but I shall know how to avenge myself. We owe each other. Don't forget it] (*CM*, 221). Malinche's words ring with dramatic irony, for we in the audience know full well that Cortés, the cad and opportunist, will sacrifice Malinche to his ambitions. He will abandon Malinche and vengeance will be exacted, if not by her hand directly, by the other players in the dramatic event, and certainly by the members of the Mexican audience who continue to revile him.

Magaña brings out that before Cortés met Malinche, he was already a "Jason," always selfishly thinking of advancing his own needs and agenda. Cortés's relations with his legal wife, Catalina la Marcaida, provide the example that his behavior pattern was set earlier, in Spain. Whereas in the Adam and Eve paradigm, Malinche as Eve bears the burden of the traitorous acts, and Adam has a less substantive role, Jason is a disreputable figure whose characterization ties him squarely to disloyalty and betrayal. Moreover, Magaña spreads the paint of inconstancy liberally among the other Spaniards, mitigating Malinche's reputation as the sole "betrayer" in this enterprise. Catalina, for example, also shows herself to be as greedy and opportunistic as her spouse. In fact, Magaña explores the opportunism not only of Cortés and his immediate family, but of the power structure he represents, that is, Carlos V. In one amusing anecdote Carlos V tries to calm the angry Catalina whose fury against Cortés relates to his mistreatment of her and his misuse of her money. In order to avoid scandal, Carlos V promises to honor Cortés and his wife with land and the title of Marqués del Valle de Oaxaca; Catalina, skeptical,

questions the emperor: "¿Promesas de rey?" [Promises of a king?].
The emperor responds to her implications by assuring her that
there is economic power behind his pretty words: "No. Letras de
Banco" [No. Bank notes] (*CM*, 213).

Moctezuma, too, appears to be not unlike Carlos V, an arrogant
and selfish monarch; he is a victim of betrayals not only from the
Malinche figure, but from the people he has mistreated: as he is
told by his minister, "Tu despotismo los acercó a Cortés" [Your
despotism led them to Cortés] (*CM*, 205). He is presented as pre-
ferring his own death if that would also punish his subjects. When
he is chastised for that selfish attitude, his response places him in
the paradigm of Louis XIV: "Después de mi, ¡el diluvio!" [After
me, the deluge!] (*CM*, 206).

Moctezuma is shown to be aware of the alliances that his subjects
have entered into with Cortés. The Indians had expressed their
willingness to help overthrow his despotic rule in their desire for
liberty, but Cortés "reads" their intentions in his own way. When
the Indians indicate they would like to negotiate with Cortés before he meets Moctezuma, Cortés interprets their reaction as an
indication that they have no loyalty to a "patria," or nation. He
reacts positively to their supposed lack of knowledge of "nationhood" with a series of syllogisms that summarize succinctly some
of the major themes of the Conquest with regard to indigenous-
Spanish tribal interactions: "He aquí, Pedro, un buen campo de
acción y un excelente mercado. Donde no hay sentido de la unión,
no puede haber lealtad, y donde no hay lealtad tampoco hay trai-
ción. Me gustan estos chicos" [I see here, Pedro, a good field of
action and an excellent market. Where there is no sense of union,
there cannot be loyalty, and where there is no loyalty, there cannot
be betrayal. I like these guys] (*CM*, 154). Within the economic
frame that Cortés places all the actions of his enterprise (the
reference to the field of action and market), he interprets the
Indians as not having a union and thus not concerned with either
loyalty or treachery. While Cortés may be misinterpreting the behavior of the Indians, he does expose his own raison d'être and
modus operandi: the search for gold, a search unencumbered by
the ethics of loyalty or love.

As I have mentioned above, Magaña does not project his vision
into the future in the same way Novo or Gorostiza did; they pre-
ferred to stress the necessity of the Conquest as the means to
bring about the formation of the future Mexican nation at the
same time they stressed the linkages between the past and the
present. Magaña, however, focuses on the motivations of what

brought Cortés to Mexico, and what the move to a different national territory means. By including Carlos V as one of the characters and by using the Medea-Jason myth as a subtext,. Magaña links events in Mexico with Europe and European colonialist traditions. Magaña exposes what he believes to have been the motivations of the Spanish enterprise in Mexico: the search for gold, the economic factors that were hidden under the veneer of a supposed spiritual and political liberation. Malinche, for example, tells Cortés that the Indians are surprised that he asks for gold and land, when he had previously spoken about a "spiritual conquest" (*CM*, 158). Cortés's response, that he wants the gold "in the name of God," is humorous, but also indicative of the economic dependency between the Church and the Crown. Moreover, when asked where his god is, Cortés's flippant response emphasizes all the more the economic nature of the Conquest and the speciousness of the spiritual quest:

> Nuestro Señor, Dios, no se presenta así como así . . . Está ocupado, posiblemente encerrado en sí mismo, como el oro está en los bancos del emperador. (Se vuelve a sus soldados) Es curioso que Dios tenga tantos bancos, digo, templos . . . pero es también indispensable; ¡es el poder manifiesto en el misterio!

> [Our Lord, God, doesn't just show himself like that . . . He is busy, possibly enclosed within himself, as the gold is in the banks of the emperor. (He turns to his soldiers) It's curious that God has so many banks, I mean, temples . . . but that is also indispensable; it is the power made manifest in the mystery!]

(CM, 159)

Magaña uses Bernal to give what could be his own perspective regarding the underlying nature of the Conquest. Bernal Díaz comments to the audience:

> ¿Qué os estaba diciendo? ah sí . . . Que una "guerra de conquista" no es una fiesta nupcial ni está necesariamente llena de chistes o de buen humor. No, no. La conquista de una tierra significa el conflicto de muchos intereses. A veces de naciones, a veces de individuos y empiezan los disgustos entre los que hacen la conquista y los que la dirigen desde lejos. (Señala hacia el área derecha) Por ejemplo el emperador.

> [What was I telling you? oh yes . . . That a "war of conquest" is not a wedding feast nor is it necessarily filled with jokes and good humor. No, no. The conquest of a land signifies the conflict of many interests. At times of nations, at times of individuals and displeasures arise

between those who make the conquest and those who direct it from
afar. (He points to the area to the right) For example, the emperor.]
                                                              (*CM*, 181)

In focusing on the Conquest as a "conflict involving many interests," Magaña offers a pragmatic rather than a romantic interpretation. He does not westernize or christianize Malinche or the
Indians, nor is he focused on the glory of the mestizo nation. He
is more interested it seems in reminding us of the tragedy that
befell the Indian nation and the issue of treachery and broken
promises that marked the enterprise. For if La Malinche is a
Medea figure and not Eve-like, then the focus is not so much on
her treachery being the initiating act or the negative effects of
the woman who acts alone and entices the unsuspecting male.
Magaña refocuses our attention on the importance of the motivations of Cortés-Jason and his use of Medea-Malinche for material gain:

Cortés. Donde hay templos hay ídolos, y donde hay ídolos, hay oro. Ya
ves qué sabia es Marina: sabe exactamente lo que buscamos.

[*Cortés*. Where there are temples, there are idols, and where there are
idols, there is gold. Now you see how knowing Marina is: she knows
exactly what we are looking for.]
                                                              (*CM*, 193)

Also, despite the importance of the infanticide in the Medea
myth, Magaña does not emphasize that aspect of the story, nor
does he focus on the production of mestizo children or their
future reincarnation as Cuauhtémoc-like carbon copies. He does
develop, however, the issue of racism, the introduction of which
is linked to the presence of the Spaniards. Although Malinche's
nursemaid lays the blame for racial consciousness on the foreigners (*CM*, 198), Cortés focuses on Pedro de Alvarado as the
guilty party for the introduction of race consciousness. When Alvarado had called Marina "una mujer de raza inferior" [a woman
of an inferior race] (*CM*, 193), Cortés admonishes him: "No em-
pecéis a propagar aquí la idea racista. Es muy útil, de acuerdo,
para después, cuando tengamos el triunfo en la mano" [Don't
begin to spread the racist idea here. It is very useful, granted, but
for later, when we have triumph in our hands] (*CM*, 193). Cortés
the pragmatist disapproves of Alvarado, but he accepts his racist
role because he sees no harm in it for him. Magaña makes good
use of the traditional characterization of Alvarado as the blond,

godlike foreigner who was nevertheless a hothead and responsible for the massacre of innocent Indians in the temple of Axayacatl. His Alvarado always mistreats the indigenous peoples and refers to their inferiority, functioning as a proto-Nazi in his Aryan blondness.

In contrast to most of the pieces on the Conquest, Magaña ends his play with the death of Moctezuma, that is, before the final defeat of the Aztecs, or the military success of the Spanish enterprise. The import of the racial wars is his focus, and the loss of liberty in the Americas which the Conquest also caused. The idea that the Conquest and the clash of cultures is to be accepted because it produced the mestizo—à la Gorostiza and Usigli—for Magaña is not sufficient justification for the destruction of the Indian nation.

Magaña's entertaining play, filled with humor, double entendres, dramatic irony, songs, contributes more than just another way of looking at the crucial event in Mexican national history. I would suggest that his use of the Medea-Jason myth as the subtext for his re-vision of the Conquest enables the twentieth-century audience to remember the racial disgrace caused by the Conquest. Instead of using the Adam and Eve topology that was most frequently used to describe the clash of cultures that engendered the Mexican nation, Magaña selects the Greek myth that focuses on the ignominy of the couple, that it is not just Medea-Malinche who is the figure of treachery, as popular culture would have it, but Cortés-Jason, and behind him Carlos V on one side of the Atlantic, Moctezuma on this side. He anticipates more the vision of Carlos Fuentes in *Todos los gatos son pardos* by suggesting that all the despots are the same, that the evil treatment of the masses will continue until the people learn to appreciate liberty. Bernal states the author's message:

(Al público) Nos vamos, es cierto y aquí termina la obra de teatro, pero esto no acaba aquí, se prolonga, se ha prolongado siempre y volver a pasar hasta que—como dijeron ellos—. . . "la racial ignominia de los pueblos se canse," o hasta que el hombre aprenda que hay algo más grande que la libertad: ¡el derecho a tenerla!

[(To the audience) We are leaving, it's true, and here ends the work of theatre, but this does not end here, it continues, it has always continued, and will continue to happen until—as they said—"racial treachery among the peoples retreats," or until man learns that there is something greater than liberty: the right to exercise it!]

(*CM*, 222)

By having Bernal face the audience and directly address the people, Magaña calls attention to the metatheatrical character of the scene, to remind them that his vision reaches beyond that of the play between "history" and "fiction," to erase the distinction between "reality" and "fiction." I believe that Magaña also attempts to eliminate any distinctions between "Old World" and "New," civilization and barbarism. Though he may say that Cortés represents a universal type but La Malinche is a local figure (*CM*, 141), his play shows that love and betrayal and death are unfortunately constants of the human enterprise.

Perhaps the most ironic aspect of his play relates to the fact that his focus on the massacre at Cholula and the Alvarado-inspired carnage in the temple anticipates the 1968 massacre at Tlatelolco. His play was presented just one year prior to that horrendous event which has also entered Mexican national consciousness as a crucial text. Those tragic deaths at Tlatelolco prove that history does repeat itself as long as the promised gift of liberty continues to be denied to the people and pragmatism and betrayal mark the political agenda. It has turned out to be another truly tragic aspect of dramatic irony for Magaña's audiences that his selection of the Medea-Jason myth—and the betrayals and death it signifies—serves as a recurring subtext in Mexico.

Notes

1. Consult Alan Riding, *Distant Neighbors: A Portrait of the Mexicans* (New York: Knopf, 1985).

2. Sergio Magaña, *Cortés y La Malinche*, in *Teatro: Moctezuma II. Cortés y La Malinche* (Mexico: Editores Mexicanos Unidos, 1985), 148. Hereafter *CM*, cited in the text. All references to the play are from this edition. Translations here and throughout this essay are mine.

3. For comments about the Castellanos and Berman plays with regard to the Conquest, consult Sandra Messinger Cypess, *La Malinche in Mexican Literature: From History to Myth* (Austin: University of Texas Press, 1991); see also the Meléndez essay in the present volume.

4. Rodolfo Usigli, *Corona de fuego*, in *Corona de sombra. Corona de fuego. Corona de luz* (Mexico: Porrúa, 1983), 129.

5. Kirsten Nigro, "Rhetoric and History in Three Mexican Plays," *Latin American Theatre Review* 21, no. 1 (1987): 70.

6. Salvador Novo, *Cuauhtémoc*, in *Teatro mexicano del siglo XX*, vol. 4, ed. Antonio Magaña Esquivel (Mexico: Fondo de Cultura Económica, 1970), 282.

7. See Cypess, *La Malinche in Mexican Literature*, 105–6.

8. Nigro, "Rhetoric and History," 69, 68.

9. Some say that the deliberate child-murder by Medea was Euripides' innovation into the saga; consult Emily A. McDermott, *Euripides' Medea: The Incarnation of Disorder* (University Park, Pa.: Pennsylvania State University Press, 1989), 12. Sarah Iles Johnston, however, argues convincingly that "fifth-century authors inherited an infanticidal Medea

from myth" and that "the Medea whom we meet in Euripides' play developed out of a folkloric paradigm that was wide-spread both in ancient Greece and in other Mediterranean countries" (page 2 of a ms. titled "Corinthian Medea and the Cult of Hera Akraia," forthcoming in *Medea,* ed. J. J. Clauss and S. I. Johnston (Princeton University Press). I want to thank Johnston for her generous assistance in providing me with her manuscripts on the subject of Medea and infanticide in ancient Greek culture.

10. Jesús Sotelo Inclán, *Malintzin (Medea americana)* (Mexico: Tiras de Colores, 1957), 45.

11. Ibid., 99.

12. Ibid., 197.

13. Jacqueline Eyring Bixler, "Re-casting the Past: The Dramatic Debunking of Mexico's 'Official' History," *Revista Hispánica Moderna* 42, no. 2 (1989): 164.

Theatre, Women, and Mexican Society: A Few Exemplary Cases

Kirsten F. Nigro
University of Cincinnati

T HE Program for Interdisciplinary Studies on Women at the prestigious Colegio de Mexico has among its many publications a book entitled *Presencia y transparencia: La mujer en la historia de México* (Presence and transparency: women in the history of Mexico).[1] The title is most revealing, as well as very pertinent to my study here, for when many of us first started our research in the late 1970s on women and the theatre in Latin America, we spoke of absences and asked ourselves just where the women were. What we thought we heard were the sounds of silence, what we thought we saw were mostly (and sadly) blank spaces. However, when our colleague Sandra M. Cypess asked "Who Has Heard Tell of Them?" and proceeded to show us that it was not a question of absences but rather of presences made transparent, of voices silenced, the task of recuperating the history of women in Latin American theatre began.[2] We still have a long way to go before the job is completed, but it is now clear that women have indeed had an important role to play in the development of their respective national stages, and that the histories of theatre that leave them out or relegate them to footnotes are biased and academically unsound in the extreme.[3] As we look at the present (tomorrow's past), it is hard to imagine that any history would ignore or underestimate the role of women who are now working in greater numbers and playing to wider audiences than ever before in most Latin American countries.

This certainly is the case in Mexico, where it can legitimately be argued that its theatre originates with the work of a woman, the nun Sor Juana Inés de la Cruz, who dazzled seventeenth-century audiences in the Vice-Royalty of New Spain with her Baroque plays of intrigue and comedies of errors. Sor Juana also

53

perfectly exemplifies the connection between women-theatre-society that I want to look at in this essay, a very complex one in which women can be both limited by the traditionally exclusionary tactics of the arts and of patriarchal society, and liberated by their subversive use of the theatrical medium to criticize and deconstruct this same society. The Mexican director Luis de Tavira has said the following: "The case of Sor Juana is without doubt an exceptional and prodigious phenomenon in the history of culture, for the quality and complexity of her work, but also for dealing with a woman born in Hispanic America, in the seventeenth century, a century and a society in which women were only domestic, courtly, religious or sexual objects. A century in which the intellectual and artistic avocation of the surprising talent of a woman like Sor Juana Ramírez had no recourse but to mask itself behind a nun."[4]

The author of various dramatic modes—*villancicos, loas, autos,* secular and religious *comedias*—Sor Juana manipulated official theatrical discourse (the only one really available to her) in order to transgress it, but in very indirect ways—Baroque, if you will—which afforded her a freedom of thought and action denied to most other women of her times. Through allegory and an ever-changing fictitious voice, Sor Juana was very often able to speak in a fashion that eluded the imprisoning binary opposition male-female; and when unable to elude it, she parodied and thereby destabilized it. According to Jean Franco, Sor Juana created spaces where she could articulate and debate questions of religious dogma, or morality and sexuality, in ways that suggested other opportunities for women and put under severe critical scrutiny the institutional codes of Colonial society.[5] In Sor Juana the so-called "disimulación mexicana" is not so much an ontological question of national or personal identity—as Nobel laureate Octavio Paz framed it in his classic study *El laberinto de la soledad* (The labyrinth of solitude)—as it is a survival strategy for a woman far more intelligent, witty, and critically perceptive than the vast majority of her male contemporaries.[6]

The academic tradition of writing theatre history (and not only of Mexico) based on playwrights makes Sor Juana seem an isolated case, for during the eighteenth and nineteenth centuries more Mexican women "did" rather than "wrote" theatre. It is the actress who now takes center stage, particularly during the long, Eurocentric reign of Porfirio Díaz (1884–1911), when she became the diva around whom the whole theatre event revolved. What needs underlining here is that despite the fact that almost all theatre productions were imported from Europe (especially Spain), Mexico did not need foreign leading actresses. The construction of the Teatro Principal in Mexico City, along with the creation of the Academia Mexicana del Arte Dramático in 1813, marked the beginning of the diva's near-century of splendor, with grand actresses such as Soledad Cordero, Merced Morales, Concha Méndez. Yet despite their important contribution to the Mexican stage, these women are usually passed over by historians of the so-called legitimate stage, who dismiss their work as too sentimental, as too operatic. Although they never say so in so many words, their subtext is that the diva and her theatre style were too emotional, that is, too feminine.

During the armed phase of the Mexican Revolution (1910–20), the social and artistic situation of women changed, sometimes in very radical ways, although their political clout was restricted until the 1950s, when they were finally given the vote. The irony here is that it was mostly the so-called revolutionary politicians who kept women from the ballot box, fearing that they would turn out to be a too conservative and pious voting bloc. But this did not keep these same politicians from using women as an essential motif in their revolutionary discourse on the homeland and the family, and from allowing women to be active participants in forging a nationalistic cultural project for postrevolutionary Mexico.

This contradiction, which kept women from the real centers of power while not denying them a role in the cultural reconstruction of Mexico, brings me back to the idea of the transparency of women's presence: they are there, but at the same time, they are not. Histories of the theatre of the period would seem to confirm this, for example, in their discussion of the Teatro de Ulises, of the Grupo de los Siete Autores, and the Comedia Mexicana, groups that in the 1920s and 1930s worked hard to revitalize the Mexican stage, the first by looking to Europe and the United States, the latter two by creating a more national tradition of dramaturgy. While there is much written about the important role of male playwrights and directors who participated in these groups, not that much has been made (until recently, at least) of the fundamental role women played in making these groups' efforts possible.[7] It was the wealthy arts patroness, Antonieta Rivas Mercado, who gave the money that made the Ulises experiment possible; it was the talented actress Virginia Fábregas who gave the cash, the theatre space, and her own acting talents to help the Grupo de los Siete Autores get started, and finally, it was the actress María Luisa Ocampo who, after winning the lottery, gave her windfall to support the Comedia Mexicana. Even less has been written about the many women playwrights who provided the scripts whose box-office success kept the Comedia Mexicana in business: for example, Catalina D'Erzell, Amalia del Castillo Ledón, Concepción Sada. And much of the little that has been written tends to dismiss them as melodramatic, as forerunners to today's soap opera writers. Thus they are more often than not considered negative influences on the Mexican theatre, present but transparent, too *femenine* for the good taste of critics and other cultural arbiters. Consequently they are erased from or slighted in the historical record, despite the fact that in their own time they were very successful, just like the divas before them.

One theatre historian who has recuperated these playwrights and insisted on their pivotal role is Ignacio Escárcega, who has said: "That unusual presence . . . of women in the Mexican theatre during one of the most significant periods of Mexico's cultural life [1920s and 1930s] would open the way for future women writers and directors, whose literary and scenic activity would have a greater recognition."[8] From the vantage point of today, some fifty years later, one must agree with Escárcega, at least quantitatively; that is, the list of women in the Mexican theatre gets longer and longer every day. But this does not mean that it is anywhere near as long as the list of men, especially in their roles as playwrights and directors. Something has changed but at the same time, it has not: again, the play of what is and is not, what is visible and yet transparent.

In the area of acting, women still dominate the Mexican scenic arts, so much so that, according to a story I was told, one quite successful playwright, when asked why his work has so many female characters, answered that because there are so many good actresses in Mexico, he can count on them to do a much better job with his plays than male actors. Even if this story is apocryphal, it serves to make an important point: that the growing number of women in the Mexican theatre does not necessarily translate into a growing concern for them per se. Earlier on I suggested that it would be hard to imagine anyone writing about Mexican theatre today without giving women considerable space. And yet, it is not inconceivable, much less impossible, for the theatre world remains very much a male-dominated domain in Mexico. Men still constitute the majority of playwrights, directors, producers, and critics. One set of statistics I have seen indicates that only twenty percent of playwrights are women, certainly a much higher percentage than in the days when Sor Juana was writing, but not high enough to claim any kind of victory. As this same study found, in a typical week, the Mexico City playbill included the names of ninety-three male authors and directors, whereas only eleven women; eighteen plays by men were directed by the playwright, but this was the case with only one of the women's plays.[9] Many of the women theatre artists with whom I have spoken in Mexico tell me that while they do not feel that being a woman has made it more difficult for them to enter the theatre world, it has made a great difference to how they are treated once there. They complain of a condescending paternalism toward their person and their work, and of the sexism which cuts them off from the centers of power and makes them vulnerable to sexual harassment. Once again, women are present, but also absent, allowed into the club, as it were, but once admitted, shunned, ignored, or belittled.

The young playwright Estela Leñero has argued that there is a need to "seriously investigate, with the help of psychology, anthropology and politics, the emotional strings and the sexist, class-based, authoritarian, snobbish and hierarchical power relations that weave themselves together in the theatre world. . . . Perhaps then . . . we can glimpse new ways of relating among ourselves and of doing theatre."[10] What Leñero underscores here is how the theatre, as an institution, duplicates or participates in social structures that are extremely prejudicial to women. And yet, because it deals with both real and possible worlds, the theatre itself can be one of the best equipped laboratories where women can dissect how these structures work, and suggest how best to break them down, both *on* and *off* stage.

Using Leñero's observations as a point of departure, I would now like to take a closer look at the work of three women working in the Mexican theatre today: Leñero herself, Sabina Berman, and Astrid Hadad. Although they are quite different in the way that they approach their craft, each of them looks through a feminist's critical eye, focusing on the many codes—social, sexual, religious, political—that have built a Mexican society where women, while ever present, are so often made to seem and feel invisible.

Of the three playwrights, Leñero has been the most realistic, creating characters very marked by their Mexican identity, especially in their language, and placing them in situations with a strong social referent. In one of her works, *Las máquinas de coser* (The sewing machines), Leñero even anticipated what would later become a real scandal when the 1985 earthquake brought down a central city building which housed an illegal sweatshop where hundreds of seamstresses worked in deplorable conditions, and whose life or death mattered less to the factory owners than retrieving their sewing machines from the building's debris. As the noted writer Elena Poniatowska has said, "Almost all of us [Mexicans] needed the earthquakes of September 19 and 20, 1985 to find out about their existence. Not so with Estela Leñero. She knew them well before. She didn't need to go down to talk at the disaster sites, to sit down on the curb in front of the fallen building and see how many seamstresses and their relatives waited for the body of a sister, of a friend to be turned over to them. . . . She became conscious of their exploitation the minute she was able to write this work . . . with a rhythm similar to the stitching of the sewing machine, the same rhythm that is imposed on the seamstresses whose every minute is clocked and who are not paid fully for the hours they work."[11]

In her play, Leñero depicts the daily work routine of sweatshop workers, one that is monotonous, repressive, and arbitrary in the way that supervisors decide who will and will not be laid off. Leñero's method is very direct in its presentation of Mexico City's working class, and she precisely captures the idiosyncratic cadences and vocabulary of their speech. The first and third scenes take place in the sweatshop; the second in a *barrio*, or neighborhood, party attended by the workers. Leñero focuses on the small details of their lives and shows how, despite their dehumanizing work conditions, they do not allow themselves to be dehumanized. The first version of the text ended with numerous workers being summarily fired, with no recourse to complaint and without the compensation due them. However, events during the September 1985 earthquake led Leñero to change the very last moments of the playtext, so that during its premier, as the fired workers were leaving, "pieces of the ceiling begin to fall down. It's quaking."[12]

In *Las máquinas de coser* Leñero continues a long tradition in Mexican theatre of coupling stage realism with social protest. However, there is an important difference here, in that the text does not suggest that solutions to economic injustice lie with official state organisms. Since the 1960s in Mexico, with the student riots and the massacre at Tlatelolco, popular belief in official solutions to national problems has become badly eroded. According to the social chronicler Carlos Monsiváis, the obvious federal corruption and ineptitude during the days following the 1985 earthquake was rather like the crowning blow, leading the general public to spontaneously organize in rescue crews that since then have given rise to political action groups at local and community levels. Monsiváis has called this "la sociedad civil que se organiza" [the civil society organizing itself], a kind of micropolitics, if you will, which represents a significant shift in a country where macro-politics, in the hands of an authoritarian state machine, has been the norm for over sixty years.[13]

The events of 1968 were also significant for the way they affected women activists who joined the student rebellions. Many of them realized that even within the ranks of Leftist rebels, the same old patriarchal hierarchies repeated themselves, relegating women to the background, where they distributed leaflets, washed dishes, and made coffee. Again, they were present, but transparent. Some analysts claim that this is what gave rise in Mexico to the so-called New Feminism, comprised of numerous autonomous groups which are not bound to or by any official structures or ideologies.[14] It is not altogether surprising, then, that in 1985 one of the first groups to come to the aid of the seamstresses was just such a group, the United Lesbians.

This new feminism could also help explain why since the 1970s much theatre written by women in Mexico has tended to focus on the particular rather than the general, on the local rather than the national, and on couples rather than families (the latter being the symbol par excellence that official rhetoric has long associated with the state). Although there are dozens of such plays to choose from, I would like to look at Sabina Berman's *Entre Villa y una mujer desnuda* (Between Villa and a naked woman), which for me is one of the most clever plays in recent years to explore male/female relationships in Mexico. What should be noted here is that unlike Leñero, Berman began her theatre career with highly experimental works, but with *Entre Villa* she moves into the more traditional form of the drawing room comedy. Leñero, on the other hand, has gone more in the direction of experimentation, most especially in her 1993 *Insomnio,* a play without words, acted within the confines of a realistic stage setting, but one that is totally enclosed by glass, making it impossible for the audience to hear anything but muffled sounds when the characters do talk. If in *Insomnio* the audience is cast in the uncomfortable role of voyeurs, in *Entre Villa* theatregoers participate more actively with their laughter of self-recognition.

Entre Villa y una mujer desnuda tells the story of Adrián, a forty-five-year-old professor of history, and of Gina, a fortyish divorcée who has been Adrián's lover for some time, always adjusting her own work schedule to his and filling in as his unpaid secretary, typing his manuscript on the life and times of Pancho Villa. In classic fashion, she is there when he needs her, but absent to him when he does not. While pretending to be perfectly happy with this liberal relationship of convenience, Gina actually wants a full-time man who will stay at home and father a child with her. While Adrián is more than willing to make babies (something easily done if she would just stop taking the pill), he is not so eager to commit to raising them. The play's four acts deal with the ups and downs of this relationship, and Gina's eventual abandonment of Adrián in favor of the much younger, inexperienced, but intensely sensitive Ismael. Adrián is left to wonder at how this could ever have happened to him, as Gina's best friend, Andrea, tries unsuccessfully (at least for the moment) to seduce him.

Obviously, this clichéd story line cannot explain why *Entre Villa* has been one of Mexico City's biggest box-office hits in recent years. Berman's real stroke of genius in this play, and what has had audiences coming back again and again, is the character of Pancho Villa, whose anachronistic appearance alongside Gina and Adrián makes their relationship theatrically and thematically so very interesting, funny, and in the end, pathetic. Berman's Pancho Villa is bewildered by this modern lover who does not just slap his woman around when she gets out of line. As he says, in his role as Adrián's mentor and coach in things romantic: "Don't let her talk, son of a bitch. Hit her, kiss her, interrupt her, tell her how cute she looks when she gets angry."[15] With his puffed up chest, high leather boots, *norteño* military garb, and misogynistic dribble, this Villa is a hilarious caricature of the classic Mexican macho at his worst (and silliest); like the historic Villa, he is someone who should be dead and buried. But in his time traveling, Berman's Villa acts as a foil to Adrián, who thinks himself so very modern and liberated. By putting these two men, of different times and social classes, together on stage, Berman effectively shows that the times have not changed that much. Adrián is living proof that a half-century later, education and a university professorship have not cured the macho of his ills. What has changed, however, is the tolerance level for this kind of behavior. Adrián and Villa are objects of audience ridicule, buffoons whose egos and phalluses are totally deflated. This is captured beautifully during Villa's final moments onstage, just after Adrián finds out about Gina's departure: "*VILLA* enters pulling a cannon. . . . *VILLA* shoots: the cannon falls to the floor. *VILLA* lifts it with his own hands and holds it up on his back. *VILLA* puts the cannon down. He's going to get up on it. He lifts the crank with great difficulty. Suddenly the cannon falls and *VILLA* comes sliding down it, falling to the floor. *VILLA*, spread-eagled on the floor. The cannon begins to make strange sounds. *VILLA* moves over to one side, the cannon's point follows him. . . . He stands up, runs, the cannon follows him. He trips, while the cannon, without having gone off, begins to smoke. *VILLA* exits, crawling on all fours."[16] After this, no more need be said about Villa's "big gun," or about Adrián's, for that matter!

Although a box-office hit, *Entre Villa y una mujer desnuda* has not left all Berman fans happy, especially some who have objected to what they consider her flirtation with commercial theatre, and a superficial treatment of serious problems. Such criticism, whether one agrees with it or not (I do not), highlights a dilemma not uncommon when women playwrights like Berman, with a voiced commitment to feminist issues, use traditional dramatic forms associated with patriarchy, such as the drawing room comedy and its contemporary offshoot, the situation comedy. There is a double bind here, also, since situation comedies so often sketch couple problems with melodramatic touches, and melodrama, as we have seen, is too often viewed critically as a minor, "feminine" art form, despite its popular success with audiences (as noted earlier, in the case of the woman-authored plays of the Comedia Mexicana).

Still, commercial success and the use of theatre forms that are considered minor by highbrow critics in general, and patriarchal by others, does not ipso facto mean that Berman has abandoned her feminist agenda. Indeed, *Entre Villa* would seem to prove that by making her theatre more accessible by being less experimental, she has reached a target audience that needs reaching: the educated upper-middle-class couples who despite all their talk to the contrary, are still very traditional in their beliefs. In conversation with the playwright, she told me of instances of husbands and boyfriends taking their partners home before the play was over, angered by the portrayal of men, and most probably, threatened by it. For others, seeing the play led to oftentimes heated post-performance discussions about the persistence of machismo in Mexican society, and significantly, about the character of Gina, who at first sight seems so very 1990s—a divorcée, a business-woman with liberal sexual mores—but who still has a pathological need for stability and for a man at her side. And while it would seem that her needs are finally fulfilled, that the play ends as all good comedies should, it is not altogether clear what awaits Gina with Ismael. On stage, he *says* many things that would signify him as the "New Mexican Male," totally macho-free, but his dress (tight blue jeans, boots, tee shirts), and his rugged good looks could lead one to wonder if with time, he will not repeat the cycle. For Villa and Adrián, each in his own fashion—one folklorically crude, the other seductively sophisticated—also have their way with words, and as so many women have learned the hard way, men's talk can be cheap.

While *Entre Villa y una mujer desnuda* provokes audience laughter right up until the curtain falls, it is not for that any less a serious statement about male-female relationships. Indeed, Berman is here following the example of one of Mexico's most eloquent and talented feminists, Rosario Castellanos, who advised her fellow "mexicanas" to use heavy doses of farce, irony, and satire in their treatment of what ails the Mexican male.[17] This good counsel has not been lost on someone like Astrid Hadad, whose sharp wit and subversive humor are making her one of Mexico's most talked about women performers.

Born of Lebanese parents, Hadad moved to Mexico City from Quintana Roo in her early teens. Raised on the rhythms of the Caribbean, she has worked the cantinas and cabarets, in routines that combine stand-up comedy, singing, dancing, outrageous costumes, off-color jokes, wordplay (the famous Mexican *albur*), and parodies of just about every sacred cow in Mexican society.[18] A lesbian and self-declared feminist, Hadad works at the periphery of mainstream Mexican theatre by choice, where she freely interprets and reworks the comic traditions of the *teatro de carpa* and Mexico's popular musical traditions, most particularly the *ranchera*, the *corrido*, and the *bolero*, all of them easy targets for her biting satire, given their inherent machismo, mythification of female virginity, and sappy romanticism. Hadad has said of her style that it is "synchretic, aesthetic, pathetic, and diuretic, where the machismo, masochism, nihilism and 'valemadrismo' inherent to all cultures are shown up for what they are, with no modesty whatsoever."[19]

While these qualities may well be inherent to any culture, Hadad's performances make them seem supremely Mexican, as in the first moment of *Heavy Nopal,* when she walks on stage, accompanied by the fanfare of her musicians, Los Tarzanes, dressed as the Aztec goddess Coatlicue, her skirt adorned with stone skulls and hands, her head graced with a charro's hat. Her face is thick with make-up, her arms are covered with bracelets, and enormous cactus leaves adorn the back of her skirt, like an Aztec cumberbund. This is a totally postmodern Coatlicue, pure kitsch and parody, a kind of prehistoric Material Girl whose every utterance and movement make a mockery of the hypocrisy that defines Mexico's sociosexual and political codes of behavior.

Hadad's work is nothing if not intertextually parodic, in the way she uses previous texts, recycles them and comes up with her own product. In *Heavy Nopal*, a good example of this is her reappropriation of the *ranchera* style popularized by Lucha Reyes in the 1940s, an aggressive, throaty, "macha" (loosely translated as masculine, perhaps even "butch") way of belting out the plaintive lyrics of the *ranchera*. In the song "Me golpeaste tanto anoche" (You hit me so much last night), for example, Hadad sings of how her lover has beaten her, but of how she cannot live without him, even if it means a lifetime of being black and blue all over. And as she sings, she puts on a bloodied head bandage, and limps around on crutches, living testimony of the damage done to women by violent men. The irony here is a result of the disjunction between the visual and the aural, between what the audience sees and what Hadad sings: the visual sign shows the ugly results for women in real life of what sounds so very bittersweet, so romantically tragic in Mexican *ranchera* music. Perhaps the most effective of Hadad's strategies in "Me golpeaste tanto anoche" is the way she makes the *ranchera* so appealing to the audience, who by being seduced by its sounds and lyrics, hopefully will also recognize its complicity in sanctioning, even mythifying, the sociocultural conditions that allow for this kind of domestic violence.

Another fine example of Hadad's parodic method is "Corazón sangrante" (Bleeding heart) from the show *¡Estalla, corazón, estalla!* (Burst, heart, burst!), which begins with two plastic hearts on stage that blink on and off like holiday lights. Against this background, Hadad quotes the Aztec description of the Conquest as a wound that hurt like having hot chili pepper rubbed into one's heart, and she ends her "story" by associating this bleeding heart with the Catholic one brought over by the conquerors. By the end of this routine, Hadad has been transmogrified into a postmodern *mater dolorosa*, wearing gold high heels, a full skirt adorned with little Aztec pyramids, a feathery head gear atop her head, a pained look on her heavily made-up face, as she unrolls a tapestry with the throbbing, luminescent heart of Catholic sainthood. The total image is a collage of sacred Mexican icons, put together in such a way as to debunk the meanings they have all accrued, meanings about suffering and self-sacrifice, about saintly and self-deprecating women who suffer in silence. It should be noted that it is these meanings and not necessarily the icons themselves that are Hadad's targets here, for in many ways, her shows are oddly enough both a celebration of what is beautiful in Mexican culture—traditional, modern, and pop—while at the same time a savage criticism of how that beauty—the signifier—can be degraded by the signifieds that are attached to it.

A common thread in this essay has been that of women's simultaneous presence and absence, of how they have always had an important role in the development of Mexican theatre but have too often been erased from the historical record. Today, with women like Estela Leñero, Sabina Berman, and Astrid Hadad, it is harder to make women invisible, especially as all three of them are not only writers, but directors, and in the case of Hadad and Berman, their own producers as well. It will not be so easy to make them "disappear." However, the terrain gained is not altogether secure; it can easily be lost by the co-optation of these women's work. That is to say, by bringing them from the fringes to the center, the powers-that-be can effectively defuse them. In Hadad's case there must certainly be an irony that a show that was presented as an alternative to the much ballyhooed and heavily government-sponsored "Mexico: Thirty Centuries of Splendor," was the *official* entry in 1995 for Mexico at the twentieth International Theatre Festival in Caracas, and was heavily attended by members of Mexico's diplomatic core in Venezuela. Berman and Leñero face the always difficult dilemma of all minority writers of whether or not to mainstream. Here I would like to sound a (personal) cautionary note, based on some of the reactions I have heard to the work all three of these playwrights voiced by fellow feminists: that it does not adhere to *supposed* notions of feminist theatre; e.g., that it is commercial, that it has a middle-class audience, that it is too realistic, that women are portrayed in negative ways, that they are not doing "serious theatre" (especially in the case of Hadad), and the like. But what should be clear by now is that there is no one feminism, that the theatre is not just one thing but many, and that if we are not careful, we ourselves who care deeply about women in the theatre will unwittingly contribute to that insidious process by which women whose presence is very real and significant are made to seem inconsequential and, therefore, too easily become invisible.

Notes

I want to thank the Taft Memorial Fund of the University of Cincinnati for grant support for my research on Mexican women and the theatre, as well as for travel funds that have allowed me to meet with many of these women and to attend the twentieth

International Theatre Festival in Caracas (April 1995) where I was able to see performances by Astrid Hadad.

1. Carmen Ramos Escandón et al. *Presencia y transparencia: La mujer en la historia de México* (Mexico: Colegio de México, 1987).
2. Sandra M. Cypess, "¿Quién ha oído hablar de ellas?" *Texto crítico* 4, no. 10 (May-August 1978): 55–64.
3. The question of how histories of Latin American theatre have been written in the past and the need for newer, more inclusive, paradigms was discussed during the meeting "Re/Writing Theater Histories: Chicano, Luso-Brazilian, Latin American, Spanish, US/Latino Theaters," at UC/Irvine in February 1992. Selected papers were published in *Gestos* 7, no. 14 (November 1992). On the question of women's theatre history, see my "Breaking [It] Up Is [Not] Hard to Do: Writing History and Women Theatre Artists in Latin America," 127–39.
4. El caso de Sor Juàna es sin duda un fenómeno excepcional y prodigioso en la historia de la cultura, por la calidad y la complejidad de su obra, pero también por tratarse de una mujer nacida en Hispanoamérica, en el siglo XVII, siglo y sociedad en que la mujer sólo era objeto doméstico, cortesano, religioso o sexual. Siglo en que la vocación intelectual y artística del talento sorprendente de una mujer como Sor Juana Ramírez no tuvo más remedio que enmascararse de monja. Luis de Tavira, "La mujer y el teatro en México. la parte," *Escénica. Nueva época* 10 (March-April 1992): 15. This and all subsequent translations from the Spanish are mine.
5. Jean Franco, "Sor Juana Explores Space," in *Plotting Women: Gender and Representation in Mexico* (New York: Columbia University Press, 1989), 23–54.
6. See Octavio Paz's *The Labyrinth of Solitude,* trans. Lysander Kemp (New York: Grove Press, 1961). Paz has also written about Sor Juana Inés de la Cruz in *Sor Juana, or, The Traps of Faith,* trans. Margaret Peden (Cambridge: Harvard University Press, 1988).
7. One such history that does focus on these women is Guillermo Schmidhuber's *El teatro mexicano en cierne: 1922–1938* (New York: Lang, 1992).
8. Esa presencia inusitada . . . de la mujer en el teatro mexicano, durante uno de los períodos más significativos de la vida cultural en México [los 1920s y 1930s] no iba sino a abrir la brecha para futuras autoras y directoras, cuya actividad literaria y escénica tendría ya un mayor reconocimiento. Ignacio Escárcega, "Presencia de la mujer en la comedia Mexicana," *Escénica. Nueva época* 9 (November-December 1991/January-February 1992): 19.
9. Coral Aguirre, "La mujer en el teatro," *Escénica. Nueva época* 10 (March-April 1992): 17–19.
10. investigar, en serio, con ayuda de la psicología, la antropología y la política, acerca de los hilos emotivos y las relaciones del poder sexistas, clasicistas, autoritarias, snobistas y jerarquizadas que se entretejen en el mundo teatral. . . . Quizá podamos . . . vislumbrar nuevas formas de relacionarnos y hacer teatro. Estela Leñero, "Mujeres y hombres en el teatro," *Escénica. Nueva época* 10 (March-April 1992): 22.
11. Casi todos necesitamos de los terremotos del 19 y 20 de septiembre de 1985 para saber de su existencia. No así Estela Leñero. Las conocía desde antes. . . . No necesitó ir a platicar al lugar de los derrumbes, sentarse en la banqueta frente al edificio desplomado y mirar cómo muchas costureras y sus familias esperaban a que les entregaran el cuerpo de su hermana, de su compañera. Tomó consciencia de su explotación el momento en que pudo escribir esta obra . . . con un ritmo parecido al pespunte de la máquina de coser, el ritmo que les exigen a las mismas costureras a quienes les cronometran el tiempo y no les pagan las horas exactas. Elena Poniatowska, introduction to performance program for *Las costureras* (Mexico: CONACULTA and INBA, 1990), 3.

66 PERSPECTIVES ON CONTEMPORARY SPANISH AMERICAN THEATRE

12. empiezan a caer pedazos de techo. Está temblando. Estela Leñero, *Las máquinas de coser* (Mexico: Universadad Autónoma Metropolitana, 1989), 142.

13. Carlos Monsiváis, *Entrada libre. Crónicas de la sociedad que se organiza* (Mexico: Biblioteca Era, 1987).

14. See, for example, Ana Lau Jaivén, *La nueva ola del feminismo en México: Consciencia y acción de la lucha de las mujeres en México* (Mexico: Editorial Planeta, 1987).

15. No la deje hablar, chingao. Péguele, bésela, interrúmpala, dígale qué chula se ve cuando se enoja. Sabina Berman, *Entre Villa y una mujer desnuda* (Mexico: SOGEM, 1992), 37.

16. *VILLA* entra jalando un cañón. . . . *VILLA* dispara: el cañón cae al suelo. *VILLA* alza por sus propias manos el cañón, lo sostiene con el lomo. . . . *VILLA* suelta el cañón. Va a montarse sobre él. Sube la manivela con enorme esfuerzo. De golpe cae el cañón y *VILLA* baja por él como por una resbaladilla y cae al suelo. *VILLA*, despasturrado *[sic]*, en el suelo. El cañón empieza a hacer ruidos raros. *VILLA* se mueve a un lado, la punta lo sigue. . . . Se para, corre, el cañón lo sigue. Tropieza: mientras el cañón, sin haberse disparado, echa humo. *VILLA* sale a gatas. *Entre Villa*, 48.

17. For English-speaking readers interested in Castellano's work, see Maureen Ahern, ed., *A Rosario Castellanos Reader* (Austin: University of Texas Press, 1988).

18. I want to thank Professor Roselyn Costantino (Pennsylvania State University-Altoona) for sharing her research on Astrid Hadad with me. Much of my background information on Hadad here comes from Costantino's unpublished essay: El arte de performance en México: Astrid Hadad y Maris Bustamante.

19. sincrético, estético, patético, y diurético, donde se muestran sin ningún pudor el machismo, masoquismo, nihilismo y valemadrismo inherentes a toda cultura. Rosa Beltrán, "Entrevista con Astrid Hadad," *La Jornada Semanal*, 16 May 1993, 16; quoted by Costantino, El arte de performance en México, 4.

Bad Girls and Good Boys in Mexican Theater in the 1990s

Ronald D. Burgess
Gettysburg College

HISPANIC culture being what it has been—which includes belonging to world culture—women have not played a very important role in Mexican drama, either as writers or as central characters. After talking about Sor Juana Inés de la Cruz, Luisa Josefina Hernández, Elena Garro, and perhaps Maruxa Vilalta, the room tends to get very quiet . . . a quiet similar to that maintained by female characters, and exemplified by Elena in Rodolfo Usigli's *El gesticulador* (The imposter): the obedient wife whose primary goal is to stand by her man. In the 1970s another equally secondary character appeared: the pregnant teen, disgraced in the eyes of her parents, usually kicked out of the house by the father, and either abandoned by the supposed boyfriend, or married to him, and hating it. While the women were basically passive, accepting, and victimized, the men were tough, macho, and convinced that they were in control. The boys were "bad" (they knew what they wanted and did whatever was necessary to get it), and the girls were "good" (they knew their place), or at worst "naughty" (usually because their boyfriends insisted, which really made them more victimized than naughty). It was not necessarily pretty, but it did reflect the times.

In the 1990s, though, a new Mexican society is beginning to emerge, at least if what is seen in Mexican theatre is to be believed. For the first time there are not only bad boys and good girls, but bad girls and, in a few instances, even good boys. This change is due, in no small part, to the emergence of plays written by women—led by Sabina Berman—plays that promise to open doors to whole new perspectives on Mexican culture. The men even seem to be following the women's lead, at least to some extent.

By 1993, after years of hard times, theatres were again featuring plays by Mexican authors, and not just by the old standbys, Emilio Carballido and Vicente Leñero. There are now new perennials, such as Sabina Berman, Jesús González Dávila, Víctor Hugo Rascón Banda, and Tomás Urtusástegui, who seem to have something playing every year. In 1993 they were joined by María Elena Aura, Leonor Azcárate, Estela Leñero, and Gabriela Ynclán on stage, and by Tomás Espinosa, Roberto Gómez Bolaños, María Luisa Medina, Sylvia Mejía, Virgilio Ariel Rivera, and Javier Trujillo Cabral in print. These comprise the most recent group of playwrights to be staged and/or published, and whose plays contain good and bad girls and boys, strong, independent women, and alternative sexual preferences. They are the latest writers to take up the struggle to bring Mexican drama back to respectability after years of decline.

Beginning in the middle to late 1960s, some two decades of hard times fell on Mexican theatre. It was a time when new Mexican plays and playwrights were criticized, ignored, or both. With time and perseverance, though, along with support from one of Mexico's premier playwrights, Emilio Carballido, and the "Nueva Dramaturgia" series of the Universidad Autónoma Metropolitana, Mexican drama slowly crawled out of the doldrums, and by the 1990s, it was again possible to find Mexican plays in theatres and, at times, even in some bookstores.

The women were crawling right along with the men, but they were fewer in number, and probably more likely to be ignored. One who was impossible to ignore, however, was Sabina Berman. By the time she had won the National Institute of Fine Art National Theatre Prize in 1979, 1981, 1982, and 1983, she was well on her way to leading the resurgence of Mexican drama as viable theatre and, in the process, establishing herself as one of the two or three most important dramatists writing in Mexico. Certainly there were other women writing, but doors generally remained closed to them, at least until the summer of 1993 when, suddenly, four women had six plays in theatres and two others were published as finalists in the playwriting competition sponsored by the Sociedad General de Escritores de Mexico (SOGEM). There are several explanations for the abrupt change, but two seem particularly important. The first is a new openness to Mexican drama on the part of producers and public, which makes it easier to recognize and accept plays written by women. The second is a wider support network, in which directors and name actors and actresses (known to the public through their work in television, in many cases) are looking for new vehicles, and find that women provide a refreshing change. Obviously the famous faces and names automatically attract an audience and make it easier for impresarios to take a chance on new productions.

Berman is gaining that kind of name recognition, especially since *Entre Villa y una mujer desnuda* (Between Villa and a naked woman) continued her string of successes and was the runaway hit of the summer of 1993. Yet Gabriela Ynclán won the SOGEM competition for that year with one of her first plays, *Coreografía* (called *Cuarteto con disfraz y serpentinas* [Quartet with costumes and streamers] in its stage version), and María Elena Aura had three plays in theatres at the same time. Leonor Azcárate's *Pasajero de medianoche* (Midnight passenger) was also playing, and *Tren nocturno a Georgia* (Night train to Georgia) by María Luisa Medina and *A punto de turrón* (Well cooked) by Sylvia Mejía were on a very short list of plays published during the first half of the year.

Success came early to Ynclán and Aura, who had done little playwriting previously. *Coreografía* looks (humorously) at two fifty- to sixty-something couples wrestling with their unhappiness and discontent. Aura's triple entrance into Mexican theatres included *La mujer rota* (The broken woman), a monologue based on a Simone de Beauvoir text, *Doble filo* (Double edged), a pair on the verge of having an affair, and *El hogar de la serpiente* (The serpent's home), the home of a fragmented and totally dysfunctional family. Berman and Azcárate have been around longer. Azcárate has been writing plays sporadically since the 1970s. Berman also began in the mid-1970s, and has only looked back to rework her prize-winning plays. Both Medina and Mejía have been involved in theatre, but primarily as actresses. Mejía was in Carballido's wildly successful *Rosa de dos aromas* in 1988. Her *A punto de turrón*, in which a wife sets out to deceive her husband's lover, reflects the humor in Carballido's play. *Tren nocturno a Georgia*, by Medina, is much more serious. It involves a case of provoked sexual harassment. A male journalism student, convinced that one of his professors is a lesbian, encourages his girlfriend to push the teacher into an action or an admission that will prove him right.

These six writers represent a wide variety of approaches and themes, but they employ some common elements, elements that help to characterize recent Mexican drama. In one way or another sex plays an important part in all of the plays mentioned. It comes in the form of sexual drives (desires and affairs past and present) or alternative sex (homosexual and lesbian relations). The latter is a relatively new addition to the stage, especially the relations between women. New also is the independent female character, the woman who is able to take control of her life and rise above her circumstances. This, in turn, makes it easier to get away from the old bad-boy/good-girl phenomenon because, especially in the newer plays, the women are strong enough to be bad. Even more innovatively, some of the men are also strong enough to be good. It may be that bad girls, good boys, and homosexual relationships could only find their way into Mexican theatre in plays by women. Whatever the reason, they create a whole new set of possibilities for both women and men.

Men, of course, continue to write, and if recent publication trends are any indication, they are beginning to feature female characters more frequently. Witness these recent titles: *¡Bety, bájate de mi nube!* (Betty, get off of my cloud!), Tomás Espinosa's mythic journey of Bety and her friend, Ana Ofelia; Roberto Gómez Bolaños's *La reina madre*, built around Charlie Chaplin's mother; *Tereso y Leopoldina*, by Willebaldo López; Virgilio Ariel Rivera's fragmented and mysterious *Madre admirable*. In *Sabor de engaño* (Taste of deceit) by Víctor Hugo Rascón Banda and *Condóminos* (Condominium dominos) by Javier Trujillo Cabral, women are on relatively even footing with the men, even though the titles do not reflect it. Despite the new limelight afforded to female characters by men, these plays are not as "daring" as the women's in three respects: the bad girl is not as apparent, the good boy is nearly nonexistent, and the alternative sex is not homosexual but incestuous. On the other hand, they do all feature a woman who is strong enough to be able to rise above her problems, and all but one involve sexual attractions.

Thus these recent Mexican plays coincide in enough ways to suggest a current trend: a focus on sexual attraction and relations, including "alternative" ones; the presence of women who have the strength to try and take control of their lives and pull themselves out of unacceptable situations; a broadening of the good-girl/bad-boy syndrome to include bad girls and good boys. Of course not all of these aspects are present in all the plays, but their occurrence is generalized enough to deserve a few brief comments to help provide a better idea of the extent to which they have insinuated themselves into Mexican drama of the nineties.[1]

Despite all the new, some things never go out of fashion: for example, that old standby, machismo, the inspiration for most of the actions that make the bad boys bad. In one guise or another it appears in almost all the plays, and finds its fullest definition in Berman's *Entre Villa y una mujer desnuda*. Although the action centers on the relationship between Gina and Adrián in the present, the presence of the Mexican Revolution's Pancho Villa as Adrián's spiritual-romantic guide determines much of the pair's interaction. The portrayal of Villa defines the macho, who gives advice such as, "No la deje hablar, chingao. Péguele, bésela, interrúmpala, dígale qué chula se ve cuando se enoja" [Damn, don't let her talk. Hit her, kiss her, interrupt her, tell her how beautiful she is when she's angry].[2] He is someone in search of physical gratification, whenever he wants and however he can get it; a tough guy who seems to feel the obligation to prove just how tough. Adrián's insistence on a relationship with no commitment reflects the demand for physical pleasure, one that is common in a number of other plays. In *Tierra caliente* (Hot land), by Azcárate, a man about to be married starts looking around even before his wedding day. The first love of one of the husbands in Ynclán's *Coreografía* is drinking, followed closely by carousing with other women. Both Charlie Chaplin and his father, in *La reina madre* by Gómez Bolaños, exemplify the roving eye, as does the main character of Víctor Hugo Rascón Banda's *Sabor de engaño*. One of the kidnappers in Azcárate's *Trabajo sucio* (Dirty work) then combines the physical expectations with the tough guy attitude, demanding sex and taking it violently. The macho is there, and has been in so many plays for so long that he hardly needs describing.

The "bad girl," on the other hand, is essentially a new arrival. She is not necessarily the female equivalent of Pancho Villa, although an interest in the physical can cast her in the role of the other woman for the roving, married macho. She is more than willing to "inter-relate" with boyfriends, husbands, and even not-quite-yet husbands, as in *Tierra caliente*. In this role she is as willing to tempt as to be tempted. She is also willing to be the cohort of the macho, which establishes another kind of badness. In *Trabajo sucio* Magda functions, for a time, as the leader of the group that kidnaps Alejandra, mistakenly thinking they can get information from her about the company for which she works. In the beginning Magda seems more than willing to stand by while Alejandra is abused, and is not above hitting her, herself. In *Tren nocturno* Dick enlists Stephanie's aid in exposing what he is convinced are the lesbian tendencies of their professor, Samantha. Stephanie later discovers that she has been duped by her boyfriend, but she initially accepts her role as temptress of the supposed lesbian teacher, eventually seduces her, and then, in order to save her own reputation, follows through in the destruction of the professor's job and reputation.

Another incarnation of the "bad girl" and a new development

brought on by the appearance of the single mother in plays, is the mother as villain, a character who takes her place alongside one of the favorite villains in earlier Mexican plays: the abusive father. She is not violent as so many of the fathers are, but like him, she has little time for her children, or simply cannot understand or get along with them. This may come as a result of having to take a position of authority in the absence of a father. Whatever the cause, she is suddenly much more in evidence. She is the workaholic mother in Azcárate's *Pasajero de medianoche,* so busy with her television career that she is unaware that her son has AIDS. She is the mother in *El hogar de la serpiente* who chose to have her two teenage boys live with their grandmother, then changes her mind and returns for them, only to complicate their lives and their attempts to understand, among other things, their sexuality and possible homosexuality. In *Entre Villa* her son is away at school, and the two are barely able to communicate, even on the phone. In *Madre admirable* by Virgilio Ariel Rivera, mother and son are again separated, but this time by choice, out of fear of the physical attraction that they feel for one another.

Interestingly enough, the woman as villain is almost exclusively a product of women. They are the ones who dare to show them pursuing, or at least enjoying, a physical relationship, to show a violent side, and to suggest that the mother figure may not be perfect. In plays by men, women may flirt and may feel attractions, but they usually respond in reaction to advances by men, in which case she remains a victim to a great extent, even though she may be a willing one. For the moment, it seems, only women are able to show that they, too, can have a negative side. The strength of character that leads to those portrayals is reflected in the form of strong, independent female characters, this time in the works of both women and men.

These strong characters fall into two general categories: those who decide to leave a bad relationship or situation instead of staying, out of fear or hope, and those who have the inner strength to transcend, to rise above their situation and become better because of it. These characters appear in plays by both men and women, and they appear in almost every play mentioned here, in one form or another.

Those who manage to extricate themselves from a bad situation can do so by simply making the decision to stand up and walk away, or they can use deception. The "madre admirable" chooses to send her son away to avoid the temptation that both feel, but neither can admit. Perla, in *Sabor de engaño,* stops letting career opportunities pass her by while she supports the macho Alfonso, and in the end she leaves him. The combination of Villa's influence on Adrián (in *Entre Villa*) and Gina's realization that the much younger Ismael can give her the love she needs finally leads her to abandon her dead-end relationship with the former and go away with the latter. Ismael makes it possible because he is one of the new "good boys" who are capable of understanding and using their heads and their hearts instead of demanding and of using only exterior, physical appendages.

Walking away is not the only way for women to take care of a bad situation, though. There is always trickery. In *Trabajo sucio* Alejandra, the kidnap victim, feigns a romantic interest in Magda. This deception leads to the death of all three kidnappers, and to Alejandra's escape. In *A punto de turrón* Sara confides in Claudia, revealing that Sara knows that her (Sara's) husband is having an affair and with whom, and that she has considered killing both him and his lover. She also describes times when he has sneaked out for surreptitious meetings. She slowly leads Claudia from complacency, to fear, to anger (all of which, of course, Claudia thinks she is hiding from Sara). Claudia's wrath is incurred since the meetings described by Sara suggest that there is yet another woman involved. Claudia's jealousy will take it from there. Sara may remain stuck with the husband, but at least she has transferred much of the problem to him and Claudia, and ensured that his fling will come to an end.

Leopoldina, in *Tereso y Leopoldina,* is locked in a business relationship with her half-brother (they have a traveling magic show) that is complicated by the sexual attraction they feel for each other. Tereso seems less capable of controlling himself than Leopoldina, so in order to prevent his advances, she tells him that she is carrying the child of one of the show's workers. While this trickery does keep Tereso at bay, it leads to other unpleasant circumstances: he kills the boy who supposedly slept with his half-sister and then, when he can no longer stand the thought of her having someone else's baby, he kills himself. When she follows suit, her triumph over a bad situation becomes hollow, at best. This kind of victory would seem to be less satisfying than the kind achieved by women who triumph through inner strength and are therefore able to carry their personal victory with them.

The women in *En el nombre de Dios* enjoy this kind of success. Berman's reworking of her earlier *Herejía* (Heresy) concerns the Carbajals, an extended family of Spanish Jews during the time of the Inquisition who come to the New World to live. All of them are outwardly Catholic in order to deceive the inquisitors, but, at least at the beginning, only the women are strong enough to carry their true faith inside, to practice their religion, and to insist openly that the men stop deceiving themselves and practice actively also. In this case the men follow the women's lead, and even though the whole family perishes at the hands of the Inquisition, they go secure in the knowledge that they have been true to themselves and to their faith. This kind of triumph is clearly more satisfying than that achieved by Leopoldina's trickery.

Lola in *Coreografía* falls somewhere in between. She stays with her alcoholic husband, Jaime, but she takes charge of the situation. They are together, but she basically refuses to maintain the relationship, devoting herself, instead, to her work. This is not the ideal situation, and Lola still suffers with her own demons, but she has stopped accepting Jaime and is able to go on about her business knowing that she has turned him into little more than a nuisance to be tolerated.

Samantha, the professor in *Tren nocturno,* is also unable to avoid the situation thrust on her by her student's deceit. She loses her job and goes to jail, after which she returns home in disgrace. Her unexpected triumph in all this is an inner peace. At the same time that Stephanie, the student, discovers that she has been used by her boyfriend, she also discovers that the only way to save her own reputation is to continue the game and destroy that of Samantha. Even though Stephanie takes this less than conscionable path, Samantha chooses to support her by lying in court, not defending herself in order to save Stephanie. The true feelings shared by the two women during their night together make the lonely Samantha's selfless act possible. Her inner knowledge allows her to rise above the viciousness of the situation, and may even bring her true love at the end, when Stephanie reappears and suggests that she and Samantha go to the United States together. Once again, the inner victories, the ones that allow characters to rise above their situation, are the only true victories.

Bety and Ana Ofelia in *¡Bety, bájate de mi nube!* also rise above their situation, literally. When the two actresses leave their plane at a stopover to search for a male companion who stupidly chose to leave the plane despite instructions to the contrary, they embark on a search for him that turns into a mythic journey in which they must overcome all manner of obstacles (some of which they conquer using the river that Ana Ofelia finds and carries with her). Their heroic insistence on sticking to their goal is done partly tongue-in-cheek, but when they return to the plane and then exit again, this time while it is in flight, they not only survive, they achieve what would seem to be happiness. In this play, as in others, the women overcome by sheer force of their own personal will. More and more frequently, though, and primarily in plays by women, the female characters also have a new ally: the "good boy."

The good boy is almost exclusively the province of women at this point. He is supportive, his strength resides in his character and not in his machismo, and he is able to show understanding and tenderness. And in most cases, his role is very reduced. In *Pasajero* he is the supportive friend of the son with AIDS. Samantha's lawyer, in *Tren nocturno*, has an equally small role, but she makes much of his understanding and his acceptance of her decision not to defend herself. Alfonso's brother, Armando, spends relatively more time on stage in *Sabor de engaño*, but his dramatic importance is minimal. His goodness arises from his virtue, his nonmachismo, so to speak. In *Entre Villa* the good boy is the younger man with whom Gina leaves, and while the character is relatively minor, he does express a different view of male-female relationships than that usually expressed by male characters. "El amor quiere ser eterno," he says, "Si no quiere ser eterno, es un amor indigno. . . . Queremos en el fondo los hombres: que alguien nos tumbe todas, todas, nuestras idiotas defensas; que alguien nos invada, nos haga suyos; nos libere de nosotros mismos" [Love wants to be eternal; if it doesn't try to be eternal, it's unworthy. . . . At heart men want someone to knock down all, every one of our ridiculous defenses, someone to take us over, to make us theirs, to free us from ourselves] (*EV*, 25). That kind of vulnerability—of expression or belief—is not a part of the standard macho package. Although this kind of character has begun to appear, he is rare, and probably will be until it becomes possible for him to be a truer reflection of society.

Likewise, alternative sexual relations have barely begun to sneak onto stage, and the homosexual ones almost exclusively in plays by women. Recently the men seem to be sticking to what would appear to be more "manly" options: incest, for example. The impulse to desire between half-brother and half-sister lies at the center of *Tereso y Leopoldina*, and the mystery that helps to sustain the dramatic tension and interest in *Madre admirable* is the hidden desire between mother and son. In neither case does incest actually occur; it is the desire that drives the action.

The women are more decisive and concrete in their depiction of homosexuality. One of the sons in *El hogar de la serpiente* finds himself wrestling with his sexual urges, trying to determine if they are homosexual or not. It plays less a part here than in *Pasajero de medianoche,* where the son is more open about his preferences. Likewise one of the husbands in *Coreografía* is finally able to admit that part of his unhappiness stems from having lived a lie. In these cases, alternative sexual preferences exist in word more than in deed. The next step is to move from talk to action, in the form of physical contact. That comes in *Trabajo sucio* and in *Tren nocturno,* in both cases in relations between women. Here, as in the case of "bad girls" and "good boys," the women are taking the most decisive steps and opening the doors to new possibilities.

As we step back and look, it would seem that the women are doing the opening, but the men are at least beginning to look through the doors. The new elements that both are introducing can only help to create more variety, produce new perspectives, and in the end, continue to make Mexican theatre more interesting. If 1993 turns out not to be a fluke, women have suddenly developed more outlets for their work, and that new force will certainly have an effect on Mexican theatre in general. Their perspectives are long overdue, and while they may be threatening, the time may be right for their acceptance. Clearly, it takes a certain amount of courage and strength to work against tradition by daring to put new characters and new actions on stage, to portray women as villains, men as anything less than macho, and to talk about sexual preferences that are not yet readily accepted. It takes a rebelliousness that comes with a bad attitude to open those doors, and it takes an attitude better than the typical macho ones to follow. With any luck, doors will continue to open, and new ideas and perspectives will continue to flow into Mexican theatre. They will, for the time being, at least, since Mexican drama currently seems to be in the good hands of bad girls and good boys.

Notes

1. The works included are recent plays that were available in Mexico in 1993, either in print, in theatres, or supplied to me in manuscript form by the dramatists. Since recent drama is the concern here, works in anthologies by Emilio Carballido and Hugo Argüelles, on sale in the summer, are not included.

2. Sabina Berman, *Entre Villa y una mujer desnuda* (Mexico: SOGEM, 1992), 36; my translation. Hereafter *EV,* cited in the text.

Rewriting the Classics: *Antígona furiosa* and the Madres de la Plaza de Mayo

Diana Taylor
Dartmouth College

> My mother lay down with my father, who was born of her belly, and thus we were begotten. And in this chain of the living and the dead, I will pay for their wrongdoings. And my own.
> —Griselda Gambaro, *Antígona furiosa*

> . . . all narrative may well be obituary in that it seeks a retrospective knowledge that comes after the end, which in human terms places it on the far side of death.
> —Elisabeth Bronfen, *Over Her Dead Body*

THE military Junta justified the coup that initiated Argentina's Dirty War (1976–1983) by arguing that the national body (conceived as the feminine *Patria,* or Motherland) was dissolving in "dissolution." From its opening proclamation to the nation following the takeover, the Junta insisted that it needed to stamp out Argentina's bad children, the "subversives" who were killing the country. The rhetoric of the armed forces pitted the authoritarian "father" against the son who threatened paternal authority and maternal integrity. Given the Oedipal narrative which the Junta used (consciously or unconsciously) to explain the political crisis, it is hardly surprising that various works of the period reflect the theme. Rather, it seems inevitable that an Antigone play should surface in relation to the Dirty War. The repeating narratives have explanatory and organizational power in interconnected social systems of representation, though traditionally we tend to think of them as divided into the seemingly separate categories of "art" and "life." The conflicts encapsulated in these stories, and the logic of their resolution, sometimes mirror each other self-consciously, but more often they seem to "ap-

77

pear" unselfconsciously in both. George Steiner, in listing the various versions of Antigone, notes that the motif comes up time and again not only in scripted form, but also spontaneously in the actions of real people:

> Even more pervasive, and altogether impossible to index, has been the role of the matter of Antigone in the actual lives of individuals and communities. It is a defining trait of western culture after Jerusalem and after Athens that in it men and women re-enact, more or less consciously, the major gestures, the exemplary symbolic motions, set before them by antique imaginings and formulations. Our realities, as it were, mime the canonic possibilities first expressed in classical art and feeling. In his diary for 17 September 1941, the German novelist and publicist Martin Raschke recounts an episode in Nazi-occupied Riga. Caught trying to sprinkle earth on the publicly exposed body of her executed brother, a young girl, entirely unpolitical in her sentiments, is asked why. She answers: "He was my brother. For me that is sufficient."[1]

The Dirty War was orchestrated by the military leaders in such a way as to exploit the foundational myths associated with nation building. They declared themselves the "supreme organ of the Nation," spoke of their commitment to create an "authentic national being" and asked that the population identify unconditionally with their heroic mission.[2] In their staging of power and order, the Junta leaders reenacted the "major gestures, the exemplary symbolic motions" referred to by Steiner. Given the narrative framework underlying their rise to power, it seems logical that opposition to that heroic scenario should also be cast in terms of "antique imaginings and formulations." Unlike the Oedipal narrative, which focuses on the male ruler's attempts to put an end to social crisis and dis*ease* through self-knowledge and the discovery of the "Truth," the Antigone story illustrates the role allotted women in the dramatic denouement. Griselda Gambaro explicitly calls attention to the fact that she will "mime the canonic possibilities first expressed in classical art and feeling"[3] in order to stage women's defiance, specifically that posed by the Madres of the Plaza de Mayo, to governmental abuse of authority. Written and premiered in Buenos Aires in 1986, shortly following the sensational "Trial" of the generals in 1985, *Antígona furiosa* looks at the Argentine tragedy after the most brutal part of it is over. *Antígona,* in which the characters speak to us from the far side of death (to paraphrase Elisabeth Bronfen's words), is both an obituary and a memento mori. It not only seeks "a retrospective knowledge that comes after the end"[4] but is a warning that civil conflict and human sacrifice seem never-ending. In the first glimpse we have of Antígona, the protagonist removes the noose from her neck and returns to life, resuscitated from death, resuscitated from and through art. Once again her presence prefigures a national tragedy of civil war, resistance and enforced absenting, the death-in-life fate of both Antígona and the disappeared.

Clearly, there are many reasons why Gambaro would choose to draw on the Antigone play to represent the atrocities of the Dirty War. Latin American playwrights have long reworked classical material, sometimes to cast national conflicts in a "tragic" light, sometimes in order to circumvent censorship.[5] But the Antigone plot specifically raises questions about political leadership and misrule, about the conflict between the so-called private and public spaces, about public fear and complicity, about a population's duty to act as a responsible witness to injustice, and about social practices and duties predicated on sexual difference that are as urgent today as they were in 441 B.C. The words in the Sophoclean text reverberate in the discourse of the Dirty War. Sophocles' Creon sounds much like the Junta leaders in his opening address when he announces the restoration of peace. "My countrymen, / The ship of state is safe."[6] He speaks of the "awesome task of setting the city's course" and adopting "the soundest policies" (l.200). He seems entirely reasonable at the beginning, and is heralded by the Chorus as "the new man for the new day" (l.174). But as in the case of the Argentine Junta, it soon becomes clear that Creon is a tyrant and that ideological bonds outweigh the rights accorded to kinship and citizenship. Creon posits that "we can establish friendships, truer than blood itself" (l.213), a position that relates closely to the Junta's version of community and nationhood: "We cannot and should not consider the marxist subversive terrorist our brother just because he was born in our Motherland. Ideologically, he has lost the honor of calling himself Argentine."[7] When Sophocles' Antigone refuses to obey Creon, she (like the *subversivos* is reduced in status to a noncitizen, even a nonperson, to "be stripped of her rights" (l.976) and banished "alive to the caverns of the dead" (l.1012). Like the *desaparecidos*, she "has no home on earth and none below / not with the living, nor with the breathless dead" (ll.941–42).

Gambaro's *Antígona furiosa* is both a quasi-faithful reworking of Sophocles' *Antigone* and a culturally specific reflection on the atrocities of the Dirty War. Gambaro uses the same plot—the fight to the death between Eteocles and Polynices, Antigone's decision to bury Polynices' exposed corpse, the argument between Creon and Haemon, Antigone's dirge, Tiresias' prophecy, and Antígona's death. She stages all this using only three characters, Coryphaeus, Antinous, and Antígona, who in turn represent the other figures, the Chorus, Creon, Tiresias, and Haemon.[8] The figure of Creon is represented by an empty shell that the different characters put on in order to give official orders—a gesture that undercuts the individuality that in Sophoclean tragedy accompanies tragic grandeur. The action of Sophocles' play (which runs 1470 lines—over sixty book pages) is telescoped into twenty pages. However, the explicit resuscitation of Antigone as the protagonist and the use of the three characters to enact all the others calls attention to the fact that this is a highly self-conscious *re*-writing. In certain parts of the play the characters recount the story, as if it had happened long ago (*Coryphaeus:* "'Then she will die, but she will not die alone,' answered Haemon," *AF,* 149); or they anticipate a famous line from the Sophoclean script (*Coryphaeus:* "He'll make use of a masterly saying." *Antinous:* "Which one?" *Coryphaeus:* "One can rule a desert beautifully alone," *AF,* 147). Gambaro's version does not adhere to the linear development of the Greek original. Antígona, for example, continues to speak and narrate the actions taking place around her well after she has died in the earlier version. The rewriting, in fact, is both the theme and the strategy of Gambaro's enterprise. She constantly maintains a back-and-forth tension between Sophocles' work and her own, indicating that it is not only the universality of the subject matter that appeals to her but the specificity of her application of it to the Argentine situation. Thus, Sophocles' meditations on misrule, on woman's defiance, on death in Thebes, provides a springboard for Gambaro's reflections on military misrule, on the Madres' movement, and on disappearance and death in Argentina. And, just as Sophocles' Chorus fails to understand the nature of the tragedy that it participates in, and blames Antigone for her own fate (i.e., "Your own blind will, your passion has destroyed you," l.962), Coryphaeus and Antinous reflect the passivity and cynicism of much of the Argentine population that opted not to interfere with the atrocity taking place around them.[9] "I don't want to see it. I've already seen too much" (*AF,* 146).

The restaging serves several functions simultaneously. For one thing, by maintaining the tension between the two historical frames, Gambaro measures the distance/proximity between the "uncivilized" world and the contemporary horror of Argentine politics. If the struggle against barbarism has obsessed Argentine intellectuals and leaders since the time of Sarmiento, *Antígona furiosa* suggests that little progress has been made. In 1853, Matthew Arnold wrote that *Antigone* had lost its relevance because its subject matter—the desecration of the dead—was too barbaric and distant an act for contemporary audiences.[10] But the distance from barbarism, Arnold and Argentina's liberal founding fathers notwithstanding, cannot be measured in terms of chronological time or geographical space. Exposing the corpses of the military's victims was only part of the Junta's horror show. Like Polynices' corpse, "an obscenity for the citizens to behold" (*A*, l.231), the bodies of the Junta's enemies were a message directed at the population as a whole. Much as in theatre, the bodies turned up as a revelation of obscene (etymologically related to off-scene, offstage) violence just beyond our field of vision. Moreover, the practice of disappearing bodies could, if anything, qualify as even more barbaric than exposing them—if ranking obscenities were the thing to do—for it precludes the very possibility of actions such as Antigone's mourning, burial rite, and defiance. The lines from *Hamlet*, the first uttered by Antígona onstage after the two *porteños* mistake her for Ophelia, further mark the distance between the past and the present:

> He is dead and gone, lady,
> He is dead and gone,
> At his head a grass-green turf,
> At his heels a stone.
>
> (*AF*, 137)

Instead of the "he is dead and gone" we have the reality of disappearance—"he" is gone and presumed dead, the terrifying ambiguous status of the Junta's enemies. Death no longer has any markers—there are no visible tombs, no headstones, no grassy plots to attest to the event.

By rewriting these deaths, Gambaro not only shows that death isn't what it used to be; art isn't what it used to be either. Its function changes as history becomes a fiction. The erasure of death contributes to the erasure of history—the move on the part of the Junta and on the part of Coryphaeus/Creon (the Junta's counterpart in Gambaro's play), of burying factual specificity under universalities: "Always fights, battles, and blood" (*AF*, 140). The word "always" suggests that violence has become normative and that people no longer recognize it as such. The Junta, as I have proposed, elevated their mission to heroic, transhistorical proportions, in part, to obscure the atrocious particulars under-writing their project. Gambaro, on the contrary, situates the universalist qualities of Sophocles' play against the all-too-factual particulars in order to highlight the latter. Reversing the classical, Aristotelian precepts, history for the Junta becomes "poetic," while tragic art, in the hands of Gambaro, becomes "historical." One of the reasons for restaging the Antigone story against the backdrop of a classical tragedy is to underline the specificity of the recomposition, the history of Argentina in the 1970s and 1980s. Death and sacrifice were not only *always* recurring, universal themes—there were very specific reasons why death and sacrifice occurred during the Dirty War. In a move to gain absolute control and stamp out all dissension, the military targeted whoever got in its way. General Iberico Saint Jean, governor of Buenos Aires, summed up the military's position two months after the coup, in May 1976: "First we will kill all the subversives; then we will kill their collaborators; then . . . their sympathizers, then . . . those who remain indifferent; and finally we will kill the timid."[11] But as I suggested at the beginning, the historical imperative of communicating real facts to a population is also linked to its flip side—the specificity of the struggle can at times best be staged and made meaningful through the use of these universally recognized symbolic gestures.

The double frame produced by yoking together the writing/rewriting also emphasizes the role of the spectator or witness in atrocity. Antígona seems to exist on a separate, distant, "tragic" plane, a dislocation made immediately evident in the play by the fact she does not know what coffee is, and which was highlighted in Laura Yusem's 1986 production by the fact that Antígona was in a pyramidal cage throughout. The other two characters occupy roles as contemporary spectators watching Antígona's ordeal and enablers who contribute to the current tragic denouement: they are "Coryphaeus" (literally, the leader of the Chorus) and his vaudevillesque sidekick named Antinous (after "the most insolent of Penelope's suitors and the first to be killed by Odysseus," respectively).[12] Sophocles is clearly concerned with the responsibility involved in seeing and knowing: "Don't you see?" Antigone asks Ismene in the opening scene (A, l.11); "how can I keep from knowing" (A, l.513), Antigone responds when Creon asks her if she knows that she must die; and the Sentry's admission that finding out about Polynices' clandestine burial puts "a terrific burden" (A, l.288) on the guards, are only a few examples of the insistence on witnessing in *Antigone*. Gambaro builds on this theme in her version, continuing her preoccupation with responsible witnessing, as opposed to what I call *dangerous seeing,* or illicit or unwilling witnessing, that spectators want to avoid because it puts them at risk. In Gambaro's *Information for Foreigners,* as I argue elsewhere, fearful spectators attempt to negate the reality of the violence they see with their own eyes by isolating it as "theatre."[13] Like an obedient audience, the population remains passive in the face of the most extreme brutality. Their leaders, after all, assure them that everything is under control. So, too, the two *porteños* watch Antígona's tragedy and fail to comprehend it as their own. They are both culturally incompetent and unreliable witnesses/spectators: "Who is that? Ophelia? (They laugh. Antígona looks at them.) Waiter, another coffee!" (*AF,* 137). They are unwilling to recognize Antígona and understand her fate in relation to the criminal politics that afflicts their society. They prefer instead to hold onto the less threatening explanation of unrequited love associated with Ophelia's death. This displacement suggests that for the Argentine, "the man in the street/café," the atrocity of the Dirty War remains, largely, unrecognizable. Like recollections of the Holocaust analyzed by Shoshana Felman and Dori Laub, the Dirty War "functions as a cultural secret which, essentially, we are still keeping from ourselves."[14] The witnesses are reluctant witnesses; they don't know and they don't want to know, for not knowing becomes the source of their sense of well-being.

Perhaps the most telling variation between Sophocles' play and Gambaro's, however, is the representation of the role of women in civil conflict. (Later in my argument, I will address the importance of the physical presentation of the character who, in Sophocles, is played by a masked male actor.) In order to explain why Antigone disappears well before the end of Sophocles' text, scholars have long suggested that she may not be the principle character of the play. H. D. F. Kitto argues that the play focuses more on Creon than on Antigone: "The last part of the *Antigone* makes no sense unless we realise that there is not one central character but two, and that of the two, the significant one to Sophocles was always Creon."[15] Simon Goldhill, in *Reading Greek Tragedy,* sums up how scholars read *Antigone* in light of the paradoxical status of women in Greek drama and society, for while "explicit ideology . . . indicates a specific linking of the women with the inside, with the house, and with a denial of public life and language, nevertheless tragedy flaunts its heroines on stage in the public eye, boldly speaking out."[16] P. Slater posits that Greek tragedy demonstrates

Athenian social pathology in its attitude toward women: "Women, repressed in life by men, find a voice through men in the institution of tragedy. The tension is, for Slater, a tension in Athenian life between the rejection or repression of women and the guilty projection of their power in the special worlds of myth and literature."[17] M. Shaw "has coined the phrase 'the female intruder' for the role of women on stage. He argues that in drama women step out of the enclosed world of the *oikos* whose values they represent, not as a psychopathological projection, but as a dramatized response to the failure of the male to respect the interests of the household in his own sphere of action, the *polis*."[18] Helene Foley calls attention to the fact that this position "fails to recognize sufficiently that a dialectical opposition puts both poles (male and female, *oikos* and *polis*) into a relation in which each defines the other." Thus, she argues, there is "no simple opposition of 'household' and 'state'"[19] in *Antigone*.

I will return to a couple of these comments, but first it seems useful to outline briefly how Gambaro's version differs from Sophocles' in regard to the status, and representation, of women. In terms of representation, Gambaro's offers a more central and human role of Antígona, who is very much the principal character. She (unlike her original) is onstage throughout, and we actually see her burying Polynices (whose body is represented only by a shroud). Through the ventriloquism of the play, she speaks many of the majestic lines that Sophocles had allotted Haemon.[20] The play starts and ends with her and her last lines indicate that she is furious at having to accept her fate of self-sacrifice: "I was born to share love, not hate. (long pause) But hate rules. (furious) The rest is silence! (She kills herself, with fury.)" (*AF,* 159). However, like her original, she both fulfills the traditional roles assigned to women in ancient Greece by washing, combing, and preparing her relative's body for burial and lamenting his death, and transgresses them by claiming a body in which the state has demonstrated proprietary interests. But Gambaro's Antígona seems more loving and vulnerable than Sophocles' heroine, against whom Normand Berlin in *The Secret Cause* has leveled charges of "inhumanity."[21] Gambaro's Antígona "turns pale" when she hears that her sister Ismene might also be condemned to death and dissociates herself from her in order to save her (*AF,* 146). She also admits that she, like everyone else in the tyrannized population, feels fear (*AF,* 144), though she refuses to be silenced by it. But more importantly, because *Antígona* is the product of such a recent sociopolitical conflict, there is a way in which the historical and symbolic function of the character differs from anything we associate with Antigone. She does not simply "represent" the interior, household spaces normally assigned to women in ancient Greece or contemporary Argentina. She does not, in the Hegelian sense, embody divine (versus human) law. While the Latin Americanist Silvia Pellarolo suggests that Antígona stands for the "rebellion of the weak" and that she is "representative of the people,"[22] it seems clear to me that Gambaro's portrayal of the *porteños* as complicitous with the tragedy makes it impossible to sustain this argument in any straightforward way. Moreover, while Pellarolo makes a passing reference to Antígona's link to the Madres of the Plaza, the gender issues so central to Gambaro's play fall out of her analysis.

Antígona furiosa, to my mind, prompts reflection on at least two of the most fundamental gender issues facing Argentine feminist writers: what are the repercussions on women of staging conflict—metaphorically and literally—on the female body? And, is it possible for women to appropriate roles and language developed by patriarchal discourse and turn them into vehicles for their own empowerment? I will explore this last question by looking both at Gambaro's allusions in this play to the Madres de la Plaza de Mayo and at the advantages and limitations she encounters in her attempts to appropriate the "masterly" words and roles of Sophocles' *Antigone.*

Gambaro, echoing the military discourse, represents the civil war as being fought on and in Antígona's flesh:

> The battle. An eruption of metallic clanging of swords, stamping of horses, screams and cries. ANTIGONA moves away. Watches from the palace. She falls to the ground, hitting her legs, rolling from one side to the other, in a rhythm that builds to a paroxysmic crescendo, as though she endures the suffering of the battle in her own flesh.
>
> (*AF,* 139)

As in the case of the *Patria,* the vision of the feminine Motherland belabored endlessly by the Junta, Antígona's body is the site of conflict—configured in both discourses as a conflict between men, between brothers (even if the Junta attempted to disqualify them as brothers and even though one-third of the disappeared were women). As President Videla of the Junta declared a few months after the coup, the *Patria* was "bleeding to death. When it most urgently needs her children, more and more of them are submerged in her blood."[23] The war was being fought in the interstices of the Mother *Patria,* in her bleeding entrails. Antígona, too, the play tells us, "endures the suffering of the battle in her own flesh" (*AF,* 139). As with the image of the *Patria,* Antígona occupies a space of mediation between men. The Junta could argue that Argentines were related and united as "authentic national beings" through their proximity to the *Patria.* This empty, feminine figure endows them with status, identity. Antígona, locked and constricted in the pyramidical cage, also mediates between and among men. Although the conflicting pulls created by the Creon/Zeus tension of the Greek version are gone, Antígona finds herself in a triangular formulation between Creon and Polynices on one hand, between Polynices and Eteocles on another, between Antinous and Coryphaeus on yet another, and between the modern reader and the Sophoclean original and between the Argentine spectator and the national tragedy on two more. She, like the "feminine" trope, is the hinge, the conduit, the empty vessel; "she" is the one that has no power but who nonetheless becomes the figure of exchange, mediation, or interaction among those who do (Creon, Zeus et al). Antígona simultaneously fulfills her mediating role and warns us against it. What happens when the female body is used as the site of political conflict? Women are trapped in roles that prove as confining as the bars on Antígona's cage. Real-life women, like the *desaparecidas* that Antígona conjures up, die violent, untimely deaths. By staging the conflict literally on Antígona's body, Gambaro stresses the connection between the metaphorical practice of staging conflict on and in the *Patria* and the fate of historical women in recent Argentine history.

But Antígona not only conjures up the *desaparecidas,* her circular movements as she makes visible the city of the dead clearly recalls the Madres' movement as well. The Madres, too, function as mediators in a triangular formulation between the paternalistic Junta and the threatening, disappeared "son." Like the Madres, who orchestrated the display of silhouettes of disappeared persons in Buenos Aires, Antígona makes the missing come to light. For both the Madres and Antígona, the dead can only be accessed through representation. Walking around an empty square, the Madres display their photographs and silhouettes. Antígona, on her bare stage, exposes the corpses on which Creon's peace and order are founded:

(Antígona walks among her dead, in a strange gait in which she falls and recovers, falls and recovers.)

Antígona: Corpses! Corpses! I walk on the dead. The dead surround me. Caress me . . . embrace me . . .

(*AF,* 140)

Antígona furiosa conjures up the image of the Madres de la Plaza de Mayo in ways that for an Argentine audience would have been immediately recognizable. Antígona's determination to give her brother's corpse a decent burial echoes the mothers' struggle to make the military government assume responsibility for their children's disappearances. In the early stages of the Madres' movement, the women haunted government offices, hospitals, and prisons looking for their missing. Estela de Carlotto, a Madre, tells how she pleaded with General Bignone in 1977 to release her daughter:

> He said that they didn't want to have prisons full of "subversives," as he called them . . . that they had to do what was necessary, by which it was clear he meant to kill them. I was now certain that Laura was dead so I asked please, would he at least return the body because I didn't want to search cemeteries amongst the anonymous graves for the body of my daughter.[24]

Soon afterwards, however, the women started walking in a circle around the Plaza de Mayo, in front of the presidential palace, or *Casa Rosada,* demanding "Aparición con vida" [Back alive!]. Both Antígona and the Madres consciously perform tragic, vaguely ahistorical roles in order to communicate the urgent nature of the civil confrontation with their fellow citizens. Antígona recognizes that she is forever trapped in the role of the self-sacrificing sister: "I will *always* want to bury Polynices. Though I a thousand times will live, and he a thousand times will die" (*AF,* 158). In *Hebe de Bonafini, memoria y esperanza,* Alejandro Diago documents how the Madres consciously put on tragic roles and icons (the lamenting woman of Greek tragedy and the Virgin Mary among them) in order to carry through with their protest. In order to protect the rights and integrity of the "private," however, both Antígona and the Madres had to renounce the *familiar* roles (in both senses of the word) historically reserved for them in society. Antígona understands that "For me there will be no wedding . . . Nor children. I will die . . . alone" (*AF* 139). So too, the Madres' activism, which stemmed from their commitment to defending their families, threw many of them into direct conflict with their husbands and other family members who refused to validate their new roles: "They say if you stop going to the square, you're one of us again."[25] Both Antígona and the Madres took to the streets, although their physical environment (as reflected by the cage on-stage) is alienating and restrictive. The *porteños* taunt .Antígona, much as Renée Epelbaum, one of the fourteen founding Madres, recalls some fellow Argentines jeering at them sometimes or, more often, crossing the street to avoid being seen close to the "madwomen" of the Plaza as they were called. Gambaro captures both of these images in the lines "Let no one come near—dare— to come near, like the mad girl / circling, circling the unburied unburied unburied corpse" (*AF,* 141). The Madres' public demon-stration of loss belied the military's assurance that everything was under control, that their fight was a "clean" fight and that punish-ment came only to those who deserved it. The women's perfor-mance, much like Antígona's, created a chain between the living and the dead. The Madres' placards showing the faces, names, and dates of disappearance of their children provided a way of re-membering the society that the Junta was trying to atomize. So, too, Antígona not only refers to memory as a "chain" (*AF,* 142) that links the living to the dead, her death reenacts that principle. Like her mother Jocasta before her, Antígona, too, dies by hanging herself. Antígona forges the chain that links the fate of women in social conflict—men seem destined for the more heroic fate of dying by the sword in direct confrontation while women, the generally silenced and unheroic victims, are forced to turn their violence in on themselves and take their own life. (We recall that Antigone's death was not the climactic moment of the Sophoclean version; the play culminates with the image of the shattered Creon walking on stage accompanying the corpse of his dead son.) Moreover, as Coryphaeus states, and as the Argentines were beginning to realize by the time this play was written: "Many women have known a similar fate. When power is affronted and limits transgressed, my girl, payment is always in the currency of blood" (*AF,* 154). One of Antígona's final indictments is directed at the population that refused to face up to the catastrophe taking place around them: "Hiding in [your] houses, devoured by fear, the plague will follow [you]" (*AF,* 155).[26]

Antígona furiosa captures not only the strength and power of oppositional movements such as the Madres', it also points to some of its contradictions. As Ross Chambers writes, oppositionality is not and never can be revolutionary because it works "*within* a system of power even as it works against it."[27] The Madres risked their lives by confronting one of the most brutal dictatorships of the twentieth century in order to protest the human rights abuses by the military government. They did not (at least initially) challenge the social system nor women's positions within it. They simply wanted their children back. If and when the Madres' positions changed, it was because they were caught in the contradiction built into their patriarchal society: as mothers, they had to look after their children; as mothers, their place was the "private," apolitical sphere. No matter how much they may have wanted to comply, the Madres clearly could not adhere to both of these conditions simultaneously. Accepting one meant abdicating the other. Thus, their decision to leave the private realm in search of their children was not, in itself, a revolutionary or radical move. They insisted that their activism was not for themselves, for their own right to be social actors or for their empowerment, but for their children. Much like the tragic heroines that Goldhill refers to, the Madres defy "explicit ideology" in times of tragedy and command the "public eye, boldly speaking out." But because they did not want to, or were not able to, challenge some of the social mores governing women's lives, the Madres were framed by the social construction of acceptable, self-abnegating "feminine" roles (lamenting mother, Virgin Mary) even as they tried to manipulate them in defense of their children. Thus, as I argue elsewhere, the Madres were trapped in a bad script, an Oedipal narrative activated by the Junta and which they themselves—no doubt unconsciously—reenacted. It is not without a certain irony that they, too, mimed the canonic possibilities of classical art when they accepted the Jocastian logo for their movement: "Our sons (hijos) gave birth to us; they left us pregnant forever."[28]

The sexual ambiguity and feminine self-abnegation underlying this aspect of the Madres' discourse finds its way into Gambaro's *Antígona* as well—whether this is a conscious reflection of the Madres' language or not is open to debate. Antígona, while embodying the political spirit of sisterhood, is simultaneously mother, love, and sister to her dead: "Antígona throws herself on [Polynices], with her own body covering him from head to toe . . . She pants as though she would revive him" (*AF*, 141). Moreover, her readiness to give herself up—body and soul—for her brother reaffirms the erasure of "feminine" individuality and specificity in Western culture, which equates individuality with masculinity. Thus, her line "I will be your body, your coffin, your earth!" (142) maps out the process of feminine disintegration—she first loses her body; she becomes the site and symbol of death (which even in this play is configured as feminine: "Death: bride, mother, sister," 156); and finally slips altogether into the vastness of "mother" earth.

The feminine, once again vacated of subjectivity, is no more than the vessel, the object (coffin or earth), housing male individuality. She, too, must sacrifice herself so that society might live. Thus Gambaro reactivates the oldest dramas in the world, "representations involving a social sacrifice of the feminine body where the death of a beautiful woman emerges as a requirement for a preservation of existing cultural norms or their regenerative modification."[29]

Nonetheless, to return to my original question, is it even possible to hope that women will empower themselves by appropriating the roles and discourse of a tradition that has historically disempowered them? Can the Madres performance of self-sacrificing women ever align human rights with women's rights? Can Gambaro, an avowed feminist, rewrite the canon or the position of women in it by taking *Antigone* and giving the woman center stage? It seems clear to me that Gambaro wants to write women's activism into her narrative. She turns the mask on Greek tragedy by having Antígona take on the role of the male heroes (Haemon, most notably), much as the male actors used to take on female roles in Attic tragedy. This ventriloquism, in Gambaro's hands, empowers women, for they now have access to an entire canon of "masterly saying(s)" and make them their own—not as echo but as a subject with agency who uses the words for her own needs. It is no longer Haemon who is furious, heroic, and individuated, but Antígona who, at least, is meant to be. It is she who dominates the discourse and—within the limits that I am exploring—uses that discourse to make her own position heard. In my reading of the play, Gambaro is conscious of the limitations imposed on women, perhaps herself most specifically. Moreover, she like Antígona is "furious" at having to live within the canonic possibilities that, seen from this anti-Steiner perspective, are as much a cage as a means of making visible. So why do it? Why speak a language that leads women inevitably—time and time again as this play indicates—to a position of self-sacrifice and silence? Because, I would answer for Gambaro, there doesn't seem to be another. Those who speak "in the voice of a woman" (*AF*, 148) are still trapped in a discursive system that cannot hear them as anything other than irrational, transgressive, "perverse," and "indomitable" (147–48). If we lived in a different universe, one that was not predicated on the gender divide which casts males as actors, movers, and doers and women as Other, death, and extremity, then this narrative would not be self-perpetuating.[30] But, as Gambaro writes in *Antígona*, "hate rules. . . . The rest is silence!" (159). Hate was the language of currency in Dirty War Argentina—the rest really was silence. Gambaro's reclaiming Antigone to portray the Dirty War was, like that character's, also an act of defiance, a defiance of the silence and memory loss dictated for Argentine society. Like the Madres with their placards or writings by the disappeared like Alicia Partnoy and Jacobo Timerman, Gambaro, too, tries to pull off a "reappearing" act. Only through art and representation, as artists and activists in Argentina committed to resistance knew, could the dead come "back alive." The three characters (like the Madres) quite literally stage absence—the other characters become visible only through them. The ventriloquism of the characters underlines that (as in Partnoy's testimonial writing) the voices of the missing can only be heard through the mouths of those who are willing to tell their stories. Recomposition, then, is the theme of *Antígona*, with all the limitations that the term implies. Recomposition through art functions as a kind of mourning—an obituary—that completes the life/death cycle and restores a sense of wholeness to the community.

Gambaro, like her Antígona, both assumes and expands on the role traditionally allotted women. In this play she mourns the deaths that took place in the Dirty War and functions as a hinge between the military atrocity and her audience in order to initiate a process of social recomposition. She goes further, though, moving into the role of authorized witness, a position that many male Latin American writers have claimed as their own. As Jean Franco writes, "the role of the one who commemorates the dead and does not permit them to be consigned to oblivion is taken by the writer who 'masculinizes' the Antigone position"[31]—that is, writers such as García Márquez, Augusto Roa Bastos, Ernesto Sábato, Carlos Fuentes, and others. Thus while Gambaro cannot change the role of Antigone, who is doomed to sacrifice herself time and again, this play expresses outrage at the discursive and representational limits placed on women. *Antígona* is not so much about some sort of mythical feminine moral superiority and self-sacrifice (another form of extremism imposed on the "feminine") as about a woman who is furious at having to continue sacrificing herself and being silenced. Gambaro works within the limits of the canonic produced by Western culture because it offers the same paradoxical visibility and invisibility that women experienced in Greek tragedy: "Women, repressed in life by men, find a voice through men in the institution of tragedy." Can feminist writers open new roads for themselves through ventriloquism?

Can mother activists continue to exploit roles that have been socially sanctioned—even invented—by patriarchal structures? Gambaro's *Antígona* suggests that we won't have answers until we have choices.

Notes

1. George Steiner, *Antigones* (Oxford: Oxford University Press, 1984), 109.

2. See the Junta's proclamation, "Proceso de Reorganización Nacional," on the front page of *La Nación* on the day they assumed power, 24 March 1976. The speech is reprinted in Oscar Troncoso's collection of documents, *El proceso de reorganización nacional: Cronología y documentación* (Buenos Aires: Centro Editor de America Latina, 1984), vol. 1, 112–16.

3. Griselda Gambaro, *Information for Foreigners: Three Plays by Griselda Gambaro*, ed. and trans. Marguerite Feitlowitz (Evanston, Ill.: Northwestern University Press, 1991). All English quotations from *Antígona furiosa*—hereafter *AF*, cited in the text—are translated by Feitlowitz unless otherwise noted, and reference numbers refer to page numbers in this edition. Unless otherwise noted, all other translations from Spanish are mine.

4. Elisabeth Bronfen, *Over Her Dead Body: Death, Femininity and the Aesthetic* (New York: Routledge, 1992), 61.

5. The meaning of the reworkings often departs from the original to directly address Latin American concerns and values. In most Latin American readings of the Antigone story, Polynices is the hero. Discussing other versions or allusions to Antigone than Gambaro's, Jean Franco notes that "the interpretation of Antigone undergoes a sea change in Latin America, where Polynices is identified with the marginalized"; in Franco, *Plotting Women: Gender and Representation in Mexico* (New York: Columbia University Press, 1989), 131. In Gambaro's play, Antígona is loyal to both her brothers, though she calls Polynices "my most beloved brother." Even Coryphaeus blames Eteocles for the civil conflict: "Eteocles didn't want to share [power]" (*Antígona*, 141, 139).

6. All references to *Antigone* are from *Sophocles: The Three Theban Plays: Antigone. Oedipus the King. Oedipus at Colonus*, trans. Robert Fagles, with introduction and notes by Barnard Knox (Middlesex: Penguin Books, 1987), l.179. Hereafter *A*, cited in the text; reference numbers refer to line numbers.

7. Daniel Frontalini and María Cristina Caiati, *El mito de la "Guerra Sucia"* (Buenos Aires: Editorial CELS, 1984), 22.

8. Silvia Pellarolo, in "Revisando el canon/la historia oficial: Griselda Gambaro y el heroismo de Antígona," *Gestos* 7 (April 1992): 79–86, sees the three characters cast as the influence of Augusto Boal's "Joker" system, in which an actor takes on several roles in order to discourage empathetic identification on the part of the audience (see Boal's *Theatre of the Oppressed*). It might also, at the same time, reflect the tradition in Attic tragedy of using three masked characters to play all the parts. Throughout this play, Gambaro draws simultaneously from classical and modern Latin American theatrical traditions.

9. Marcelo M. Suárez-Orozco, in "The Heritage of Enduring a 'Dirty War': Psychological Aspects of Terror in Argentina, 1976–1988," *Journal of Psychohistory* 18, no. 4 (1991), writes that "the great majority of Argentines . . . developed conscious and unconscious strategies of knowing what not to know about events in their immediate environment" (469).

10. See Knox's introduction to *Sophocles: Three Theban Plays*, 35.

11. Quoted in John Simpson and Jana Bennett, *The Disappeared: Voices from a Secret War* (London: Robson Books, 1985), 66.

12. See Edward Tripp, *The Meridian Handbook of Classical Mythology* (New York: New American Library, 1970), 55. Pellarolo explains the specific Argentine flavor of the two

characters by relating them to a figure originating in the tango—the "el vivo" [the wiseguy] who develops from "el guapo" [the good-looker], the inflexible *macho* who toughs out his insecurity and cowardliness ("Revisando el canon," 82).

13. See Diana Taylor, "Theatre and Terrorism: Griselda Gambaro's *Information for Foreigners*," *Theatre Journal* 42, no. 2 (May 1990): 165–82, and Diana Taylor, *Theatre of Crisis: Drama and Politics in Latin America* (Lexington: University Press of Kentucky, 1991), chap. 3.

14. Shoshana Felman and Dori Laub, *Testimony: Crisis of Witnessing in Literature, Psychoanalysis, and History* (New York: Routledge, 1992), xix.

15. H. D. F. Kitto, *Greek Tragedy* (New York: Doubleday, 1954), 130.

16. Simon Goldhill, ed., *Reading Greek Tragedy* (Cambridge: Cambridge University Press, 1986), 113.

17. Ibid.

18. Ibid.

19. Ibid., 114.

20. Pellarolo notes that Antígona speaks some of Haemon's lines ("Revisandro el canon," 83), but she fails to consider that Antígona is actually "playing" Haemon when she does so, a fact that sets up a complex and interesting ventriloquism that she fails to notice.

21. Normand Berlin, *The Secret Cause: A Discussion of Tragedy* (Amherst: University of Massachusetts Press, 1981), 21.

22. Pellarolo, "Revisando el canon," 79, 80.

23. Troncoso, *El proceso de reorganización*, 1:59.

24. Jo Fisher, *Mothers of the Disappeared* (Boston: South End Press, 1989), 20.

25. Ibid., 156.

26. Feitlowitz translates this as "Hiding in *our* houses, devoured by fear, the plague will follow *us*" (emphasis added), but "your" and "you" are the faithful translation of "Escondidos en sus casas, devorados por el miedo, los seguirá la peste" (*Antígona*, 214). The "you" also makes more sense in terms of the scene, for Antígona has already offered up her flesh to the carrion-feeders and has accepted the responsibility of living in a society contaminated by violence and fear.

27. Ross Chambers, *Room for Maneuver: Reading (the) Oppositional (in) Narrative* (Chicago: University of Chicago Press, 1991), xvii.

28. Alejandro Diago, *Hebe Bonafini: Memoria y esperanza* (Buenos Aires: Ediciones Dialectica, 1988), 119.

29. Bronfen, *Over Her Dead Body*, 181.

30. Bronfen notes how Western culture associates women with extremity: "Woman comes to represent the margins or extremes of the norm—the extremely good, pure and helpless, or the extremely dangerous, chaotic and seductive (ibid.).

31. Franco, *Plotting Women*, 131.

The Theatre of Roberto Cossa:
A World of Broken Dreams

George Woodyard
University of Kansas

R OBERTO Cossa has been quoted as saying that "me gustaría que me recordasen como un autor cuyos textos ayudaron a comprender nuestra realidad y nuestra irrealidad" [he would like to be remembered as an author whose texts helped to understand our reality and our irreality].[1] Now the senior member of his generation of Argentine playwrights responsible for unusual growth, Cossa has balanced his theatre between considerations of aesthetics and form and his concern over sociopolitical issues in his country.

Born into a middle-class family, Cossa grew up with a strong sense of family values in the ethnically mixed neighborhood of Villa del Parque.[2] Upon finishing at the Colegio Nacional Secundario in 1953, he began studies in medicine but left the program after a year. When his family moved to San Isidro, he joined the local theatre group, the Teatro Independiente de San Isidro, where he experimented with acting and directing until he discovered his real interest lay in writing for the theatre.

Strongly influenced by North American and European playwrights, especially Arthur Miller and Anton Chekhov, Cossa began to write under the moral and social impact of such plays as *Death of a Salesman* and *The Cherry Orchard*. The techniques and politics of both were inspirational not only to Cossa but to others of his generation. Cossa's concerns about life, society, and politics led to plays that express the inability of the people to create and sustain a government that serves its needs because of the character flaws within the people themselves. These problems are deeply embedded in the fabric of Argentine culture, given its formative history. Although many working-class people immigrated to Argentina to escape the grinding poverty of their native lands, many

94

of them thought to return to Europe once their fortunes were secure. Further, the upward mobility that was possible in this land of opportunity where the children of workers could achieve professional status as doctors, attorneys, or engineers created a sense of easy prosperity. The reality that accompanied both of these major factors was not always so pleasant. Cossa's theatre has constant reminders of the illusory quality of life, coupled with a sense of nostalgia for the better days of yesteryear. Through a wide variety of techniques (e.g., watching television, eating and drinking to excess) that Donald Yates calls "conscience-numbing remedies,"[3] his characters seek to disguise or avoid the reality that is otherwise too painful to confront. Even so, Cossa handles his characters with a gentle and intimate touch, as Luis Ordaz has observed,[4] seeking ways to express their anguish in a twentieth-century world. Osvaldo Pellettieri refers to this period as the "jerarquía del personaje mediocre" [hierarchy of the mediocre character],[5] a lesson well learned from Miller's *Death of a Salesman*.

The plays in volume one of Cossa's *Teatro*[6] depend on realistic techniques that reveal the general malaise of different groups or individuals at odds with the society, themselves, or another generation. Cossa establishes a pattern of short to full-length plays, some with playful titles, that engage in characterization at fundamental levels. His first play, *Nuestro fin de semana* (Our weekend, 1964), sets the parameters of his realistic theatre. Focusing on a group of people in their thirties and forties, he paints a cross-section of *porteño* society at the time. The focal point is a weekend house, supposedly a place of relaxation and camaraderie among good friends. Beneath the surface, however, lie the anguish, frustrations, solitude, and despair of individuals whose lives are economically uncertain and who seek solace in memories of yesteryear when families and times were secure. The clear image that emerges is that of a country in which opportunities are limited, business ventures fail, and people live with nerves on edge, seeking escape through weekends of debauchery in futile exercises of self-indulgence. This first play is significant because it establishes the parameters of Cossa's theatre in which he reveals his capacity to develop believable characters, write strong dialogue, and portray people within lifelike situations that characterize contemporary Buenos Aires during a difficult period. The images of a previous time when the city offered greater hope to its young people and greater security to the working classes are imbedded even within this first play.

The realistic tendency continues in *Los días de Julián Bisbal* (The days of Julián Bisbal, 1966) through a focus on a young man who suffers an enormous sense of alienation. With an episodic structure in six scenes it provides insights into the *porteño* character of the mid-1960s through deliberate exposition of an individual whose employment offers neither challenge nor growth, and for whom life has become meaningless. Married too young, dissatisfied with his wife, discouraged and envious as a result of contacts with former friends, Julián seeks to assuage his frustrations by making contact with an earlier girlfriend, now a reluctant prostitute. At the end of the day he returns home to his wife, dejected but resigned to the only human contact that he has available to him. By setting up paradigmatic situations in which Julián's attitudes and behaviors are contrasted with others, Cossa reveals the depth of despair of this victim of "la fiaca,'' to borrow Ricardo Talesnik's term. Cossa's portrait of the Argentinian of his generation is bleak and disheartening with obvious residuals from the society.

La ñata contra el libro (Nose against the book, 1966) continues the theme of frustration and disengagement in a brief one-act play whose central character, David Belmes, intends to win the million peso prize offered by Gotán for the best tango. (Gotán was an important Buenos Aires *tanguería*, now closed.) The title derives from a famous tango by Enrique Santos Discépolo, "la ñata contra el vidrio," that is, the little boy with his nose against the window, too young to enter but dreaming wistfully of another world. Cossa's modification signals the intellectual and cultural formation that he finds lacking in *porteño* culture. Pathetically, the central character wishes for the big prize but has neither the life experience nor the intellectual resources to meet his goal. While the Announcer maintains a running commentary that creates dramatic tension for meeting the deadline, David wastes his time in futile speculation about a suitable theme, thus revealing the shallowness of his character and, more importantly, the disjuncture between his dreams and illusions as measured against his sense of commitment and creative abilities. If the cultural ethos is predicated on winning the lottery, instead of working toward goals and objectives with dedication and purpose, as Cossa appears to be saying, it bodes poorly for national development and stability.

In *La pata de la sota* (The foot of the knight, 1967) Cossa ventures for the first time into temporal dislocations. Although set in 1966, the action repeatedly flashes back to four to six years earlier, a technique that was not entirely successful because of the diffi-

culty in identifying on stage the time boundaries. The play continues the trajectory by now well established in Cossa's writing of
portraying middle-class disillusions, as seen through a couple
whose dreams of advancement and fulfillment for their children
come to frustration and despair. From the parents' vantage point
of an ethical posture rooted in hard work, honesty, decency, and
religious beliefs, they watch their three children chase financial,
political, and amorous chimeras that bring heartbreak and despair. Imbedded in this syndrome of generational conflict is a
message about changing value systems, the loss of a work ethic,
and a devotion to easy success through get-rich-quick schemes or
easy liaisons. With its title and central image related to card playing, an allusion to slowly revealing the cards, the play reveals basic
perceptions about a society in the process of disintegration.

Tute cabrero (1981) continues a similar motif through reference
to a popular card game for three persons in which the objective
is to have either most or least points, with the person in the middle
losing. The metaphor captures perfectly a factory situation in
which management decides that three employees must choose
among themselves which one of them is to be dismissed. The play
offers compelling dynamics among the three men and the women
in their lives (one wife, one sister, one lover), all directed toward
questions about aging, competence, pride, and group solidarity.
Cossa manipulates music and intercalated time scenes into more
complex arrangements than previously seen in his plays.

The second published volume overall is more experimental;
with only three plays it marks a significant new point of view with
new approaches. The first play of the volume is *El avión negro*; its
premiere coincides with the new decade of the 1970s. Because of
its collaborative modality, written by Cossa, Germán Rozenmacher,
Carlos Somigliana, and Ricardo Talesnik, it is nearly unprece-
dented as a theatre piece, yet paradoxically it typifies the collaboration that regularly takes place among Argentine writers. When
their discussion turned to the return of Juan B. Perón, exiled in
Madrid since 1955, the project took shape as the four wrote segments without pride of authorship in order to compile an over-
view of sociopolitical attitudes regarding Peronist politics. The
result was a work that Ricardo Halac identifies with the Argentine
grotesque.[7] The play is a virtual documentary in future time; it
projects a "new 17th," a reincarnation of the celebrated day of
Perón's ascension to power. The play is both fragmented and unified: through the twelve episodic scenes the *murga* [crowd] provides the unifying thread, a parade of *descamisados* [shirtless ones],

winding through the play as a parade during carnival, heralding the dictator's return. The scenes reveal actions and attitudes: the materialistic bourgeoisie, the reactionary professional groups, the rhetorical clergy, and the old-style revolutionaries. On the other hand, the protestors themselves are inept, hypocritical, and uncertain of their goals. Lucho, the drummer, sets the rhythmical pace with his drum, a motif that explodes into a deafening roar at the end of the play as two establishment officials facetiously tout "amor, mucho amor, mucha fe" [love, lots of love, great faith] as they brutally dismantle a blue-collar puppet ("un negro") to protect the society from "caos . . . ni inmoralidad . . . ni violencia" (2:66). The lively action and dialogue are interspersed with original lyrics set to traditional tunes. The tone is variable: at times tender and pathetic, often humorous, both in dialogue and action (with a great deal of black humor), and often brutal. The techniques of physical torture, interrogation, brutality, nudity, sexuality, profanity, interchangeable identities, and puppets support the central criticism with the threat—or the promise—of a popular revolt.[8]

When myth became reality and Perón actually returned to Argentina in 1974, political strife became increasingly rampant, and Cossa was silent until 1977 when *La nona* was staged in the Teatro Lasalle. Without question Cossa's most popular work, a play translated and performed widely throughout Latin America and Europe, it stands as another indictment of the middle class for failing to adapt to a changing reality or to make serious efforts to improve it. As economic conditions deteriorate, putting increased pressures on the family structure, each person either neglects to act or reacts in ways inappropriate to the crisis. As a result, all die or leave by the end of the play, with the exception of the titular character, La Nona, the 100-year-old grandmother with an insatiable appetite who literally eats them out of house and home. As a metaphorical representation of a society run amok, La Nona signifies voraciousness to the point of annihilation. Instead of addressing the problem at the source, the family seeks fanciful ways to maintain the budget. The person most guilty of neglect is the brother, whose creativity for finding solutions to the Nona problem, in order to avoid going to work, far exceeds his creativity for composing tangos. The young daughter slips into prostitution; the aunt has no viable earning power. If *El avión negro* represents the grotesque, *La nona* is a nearly perfect example of Halac's definition: "premisas ideológicas claras, personajes marcados por un rasgo grueso—que no excluye los matices—; diálogo directo;

tono tragicómico, que empieza en la farsa y termina en una revelación dramática; búsqueda del espectador para conmoverlo" [clear ideological premises, broad-brush characterization—which does not exclude tones; direct dialogue; tragicomic tone that begins in farce and ends in a dramatic revelation; an effort to touch the audience emotionally].[9] *La nona* depends on techniques of the absurd with gross humor throughout. The inability of the family unit to respond meaningfully to its problems signals the crisis in the value system within the middle-class Argentine society that Cossa describes so effectively.

Cossa finished out the decade, now passing through the worst period of the Dirty War, with *No hay que llorar* (No need to cry, 1979). Whereas *La nona* projected an image of a society out of control, ravishingly hungry, and ravaging everything in sight, this play succeeds with a similarly chilling motif. At a family gathering to celebrate the Mother's birthday, the Mother becomes ill; when she recuses herself, the three children discover the documentation of property she owns. Their fantasies about sudden riches bring disastrous results for the infirm Mother. Just as in *La nona*, food and drink play a major role in the dramatic structure of the play. The dominant themes of the play are avarice, jealousy, vengeance, and small martyrdoms, all of which are equivalent to a total breakdown of the value system within this family, itself a microcosmic representation of the society. The sounds of the famous tango, "El caminito," are heard throughout the play; as one of the best-known tangos, based on a short street in Buenos Aires, Caminito en la Boca, it provides musical relief and at the same time a unifying thread.

By the 1980s Cossa's theatre enters a new phase, becoming more overtly politicized. The allusions and images of his earlier plays were never lost on an Argentine public, but the deterioration in the social fabric of the country during the late 1970s, with the imposition of the military regime and the "disappeared ones" of Argentina's Dirty War, provoked a stronger response to Cossa's theatre. The first play of the third volume is *El viejo criado* (The old servant, 1979), a play that anticipates his new orientation. References to Jimmy Carter, Leandro Alem, Kant, Keynes, Kropotkin, Perón, all of whom represented illusions of a better society at critical junctures, underscore the turbulence of the political situation. The search for a "viejo criado" who will take care of everything, a metaphorical panacea for everything wrong with the people and the society, provides the dramatic impulse for this play with its strong sense of nostalgia for past times of greater stability. The monotony of repeated actions is offset by the stability and reassuring nature of such actions. The permanence of the trio, the sameness of the stories, the constancy of the search— all are qualities that characterize the dreams and glories of times past. The two central figures represent classic divisions in Cossa's theatre between the coarse, rough type and the pseudo-intellectual. When Carlitos (in search of the perfect tango) returns from Paris with Madame Yvonne, the French prostitute who at first refuses to tell her story, the references conjure up images of the golden dream that Paris represents and to the famous tango "Madama Yvonne." She arrives in Argentina with her own sense of "morality" which degenerates as she comes in contact with the corruptness of the local society. Her downward spiral from point of entry stands as eloquent testimony to the degradation of local politics and economics. In this pathetic and antiquated environment, in which everybody wants to be a somebody, Cossa creates a metaphor for a wasted society that lives with its myths and illusions, trying to recapture former glories. *El viejo criado* sets the tone that characterizes his theatre of the 1980s.

In 1981, with the country gripped in the depths of military oppression, the country's playwrights and directors rallied around a dramatic challenge organized primarily by Osvaldo Dragún under the aegis of Teatro Abierto [Open Theatre]. The objectives of showing solidarity and resistance against the madness of the current government were accomplished through the twenty-one plays that demonstrated not only the vitality of the playwrights but the ingeniousness of the directors who staged these one-act plays at a pace of three each night. Cossa contributed a piece dedicated to his friend Carlos Somigliana for his help with the title, taken also from a famous tango ("canzoneta"). *Gris de ausencia* (Gray is for absence, 1981) deals with the burgeoning problem of the Argentine diaspora, an issue that had reached astonishing and demoralizing proportions. The situation is both humorous and pathetic as members of the same family attempt to communicate with each other across national boundaries in different languages, a situation that is punctuated with grotesque humor in order to make its political point: if it were not for the atrocities of the Argentine political system, these families would not suffer the anguish caused by exile. The play presents a satirical view, in that long tradition of the grotesque creole style, of a disturbing dimension of Argentine life.

The next year Cossa premiered *Ya nadie recuerda a Frederic*

Chopin (Nobody remembers Frederic Chopin anymore, 1981–1982). Much like the previous plays, this one makes its strong commentary about repressive systems and people who live with illusions of the past. The primary action takes place in two locations and in two time registers, past and present, between the time of the Spanish Civil War and World War II, both with their cataclysmic upheavals. The many political references throughout the play point to the insidious nature of political extremism, either on the right or the left. The main characters are caught in a world of illusions; the mother fantasizes that her daughters will play piano, speak French, and be ballerinas. The repeated references to Margarita Xirgu coming to dinner provide faded and delusionary images of fame by association. Frank, a confused anarchist/socialist, roams the world in search of women with big bosoms, thus calling into ridicule his political inclinations. More than Cossa's previous plays, this one involves some magical realism, including trains that will not stop and people who will not get off. The principal fantasy belongs to the mother, who lives with the illusion that the cemeteries in France are filled on 17 October with people honoring the memory of Chopin (1810–1840), although Frank shatters her illusions about this fateful day, the anniversary of the day Perón was liberated from prison by popular demand in 1945.[10]

El tío loco (The crazy uncle, no date) imparts much of the frenetic pace characteristic of many Cossa plays. Without any extraordinary techniques the play highlights the pathetic nature of the human condition under duress. The setting is a dilapidated house where the family engages in one of Cossa's favorite dramatic pastimes—eating and drinking to excess, even though it is clear the family is passing through difficult financial times. In order to meet expenses they have opened a kiosk out the back window, and they are caring for children and old people in the house; all of these intrusions exacerbate family tensions. The arrival of the Tío Loco, returning to the neighborhood after a forty-year absence, provides a brief, entertaining, and even erotic interlude before he dies in the arms of his only good friend, a German drinking buddy with whom, pathetically, he has no common language. For the family the uncle represents a carefree lifestyle; for the uncle the family represents stability. For both the images are as artificial as the society that has created them. The most pathetic image of all in this sad and beguiling play is that of the parents, who are encouraging the young daughter to be a "vedette" against her wishes because of the glamour and success it can bring.

De pies y manos (from the expression, "atado de pies y manos," i.e., bound hand and foot, 1984) strikes another blow at the pretensions of Argentine society by focusing on a young man trapped by the artificiality of those around him. The central motif uniting a strange assortment of personalities is the ubiquitous card game they play, a useless pastime that brings people together but not necessarily within a spirit of solidarity. Miguel attempts to function as the unifying element, but the results are questionable because of the irrational behaviors of others. When the society is artificial and perverse (exemplified particularly by the totally pastiche girlfriend with her false hair, eyelashes, nails, and even breasts), piety is of little value. As the central figure, he is beleaguered by the demands of his friends and relatives, to the point that he becomes immobilized. As in previous examples, the metaphorical implications regarding Argentine society and politics of the time are imbedded in the text.

In the Lorange Theatre in 1987 Omar Grasso staged *Yepeto*, unquestionably Cossa's most complex work to date, which presents an intriguing case of literary intertextuality with a focus on the interrelationships of art, music, literature, and theatre. As the title indicates, *Yepeto* derives from a relationship between what Gennette calls the current hypertext and its hypotext, the novel *Pinocchio* by the famous nineteenth-century Italian writer Carlo Lorenzini, alias Collodi. Although the image of the puppeteer and his little creation has evolved greatly during the twentieth century, the fundamental characteristics remain intact, i.e., the capacity of the creator to mold, teach, and help his creation. Based on the ancient formula of the amorous triangle, the play depends on the competition between two men for one woman. A young athletic student, Antonio, accuses the fiftyish professor of wanting to seduce his girlfriend, the professor's student. Cecilia, although physically absent, is the catalyst for the action between the two men. The action is framed by the parallel internal story the professor is writing, a triangular love affair involving a young woman attracted intellectually to her tutor and physically to a young Hussar lieutenant, with parallel references to Shakespeare's Othello, Desdemona, and Iago and Victor Hugo's Jean Valjean, Cosette, and Mario. At the end the professor's cynical comment, "me cago en la literatura" [fuck literature] (3:241), indicates his desperation about either creating a story or identifying a happy relationship for himself.

The absent figure, a well-known technique in Argentine theatre, is key to the work and confirms the concepts of power. As a creation of the professor, the young woman functions as a puppet of the two men—at times a victim of their erotic desires, at times in control of the formula. By deconstructing what the two say (our only source of information in that she exists only as a projection of their personalities), we perceive a kind of dramatic "performance" based on their own necessities. The internal changes of tone and perspective channel the rhythm of the play into a dramatic *pas de deux* until the professor is revealed as "Gepeto," the puppeteer/creator, leaving him vulnerable to Antonio's insults. For the professor this is the ultimate debasement, an indication that the created has reached stature equivalent to the creator.

The play in its totality presents the image of a man distressed by advancing age and his diminishing capacities as a writer, lover, and human being. The insistence on youth, which he links with creativity, is key to his anguish. Throughout, the main concept is *control.* The professor tries to control his creations, i.e., Cecilia, and even Antonio. Control, or the lack of it, motivates the work, giving it social dimensions as well, just as in the original *Pinocchio.* The occasional references to the Malvinas also underscore the importance of control within the society. The extraordinary quality of this play is the subtlety with which Cossa handles the intertextual construction in commenting on fundamental human problems along with social commentary about Buenos Aires and its inhabitants.

The same year, 1987, Cossa's *El sur y después* (The South and later) opened in the Teatro de la Campana. Directed by José Bove, the play emerged as a collective experiment in which Cossa collaborated with the students in Bove's Municipal Dramatic Art School and three other young authors. Another one-act play with multiple characters, this one is notable for the frenzied pace of its trains running north and south in the years following the War of the Malvinas. The perverse or even demented characters in the station waiting to board the train of life, as it were, typify a range of disillusioned, disconnected individuals, caught in a web of memories and forgetfulness, unable to identify with processes of change. The "south" is representative of the marginalized classes and individuals whose dreams and fantasies include boarding the trains to the "north," itself symbolic of a return to stability and prosperity. This chaotic little play is saturated with representations of popular culture, including appropriate tangos and songs.

The fourth volume of Cossa's *Teatro,* the last published to date, contains three quite different plays that mark levels of experimentation previously unseen in Cossa. One play is a musical comedy;

a second is predicated on a documented historical episode; the third is an adaptation of a classical French play.

Cossa had drafted *Angelito* (Little angel) as early as 1986, but it lay in the drawer until 1991 when Luis Macchi urged him to complete it. In the immediate aftermath of the fall of the communist state, the play seems especially poignant for its political posture. The central character is a "revolutionary" who agitates for the causes of socialism but encounters many distractions along the way. Set in the form of a musical comedy, the entire play is written in verse, Cossa's first, with segments designated as musical interludes. The six women in the play represent different political postures as they serve to complement the range of human emotions and vices that detract both men and women from their appointed goals. While the excesses of capitalism and communism run rampant through the thematic core of the play, socialism appears at the desired center, but it is difficult to achieve because of the weaknesses of the human spirit. "Wine, women and song" could be a fair description of the distractions that are couched in jocular terms, along with the self-doubts about the effectiveness of the political campaigns. Even the protest march with massive participation becomes suspect. As the *Responsable* sings:

> Bien compañeros . . .
> Hemos comprobado una verdad.
> El socialismo es un arma
> para cambiar la realidad.
> Bienvenida la imaginación
> siempre y cuando
> sea ciencia y no ficción.

> [Well, friends . . .
> We have established the truth.
> Socialism is a weapon
> for changing reality.
> Imagination is welcome
> just as long as
> it is science and not fiction.]

(4:115)

If *Angelito* does not represent a major landmark within Cossa's dramaturgy, it does mark a significant new level of experimentation.

With *Los compadritos* (The buddies, 1985) Cossa departed from a historical event. Staged in the Teatro Municipal Presidente Alvear and directed by Villanueva Cosse and Roberto Castro, the play is set in 1939 after the sinking of the German U-boat Graf Spee off the coast of Uruguay. The six scenes correspond to the years up through 1945 with an epilogue in present time, i.e., forty years later. Based on the sudden and startling appearance of two German survivors at a poor beach bar, the play documents a vision of social and political opportunism. The bar owners indicate their faith and belief in the promised triumph of the Third Reich by exploiting the presence of the Germans to enhance their business and by marrying their daughter, an aspiring ballerina, to one of them as virtual collateral. Before Argentina declares war against the Axis and the system collapses, they engage in the search for a proper Argentine hero/mascot to symbolize the struggle they will take to the streets. For numerous reasons both Juan Manuel de Rosas and Gardel are rejected, thus making room for an un-named contemporary figure, an assumed reference to Perón. The postdated epilogue stands as eloquent testimony to how little has changed through the figure of the now forty-year-old son hysteri-cally demanding control and order, reminiscent of his fascist fa-ther. The intervention of the *morocho* is brief but significant because it epitomizes the title, "los compadritos," that is, the "bud-dies" who stick together, impervious to the political winds. The professor is also a classic case of vacillation, willing to champion any cause that brings personal benefit. Throughout the play only Steiner stands firm in his deformed beliefs; all the others willingly sell their value systems for whatever materialistic or status ad-vantage they can acquire. This fictional version of an histori-cal episode does little to conceal Cossa's cynicism about personal integrity.

In 1986 Cossa collaborated with Julio Ardiles Gray in a new translation and adaptation of Molière's *Tartuffe,* making some modifications in the text. While the core characters remain the same, following the same essential story line, this version can in no way be considered a mere translation from French to Spanish. Without reference to setting, time or place, the play advances the characterization of the avaricious, lecherous Tartufo, who gradu-ally lays claim to everything in Orgon's house and household, including Orgon's promise of his daughter, Mariana, in marriage. The revelation that Tartufo is, in fact, a lecher capable of seducing his wife finally brings Orgon to his senses, but not before Orgon has transferred his property to Tartufo. The legal obligation to vacate the premises is obviated at the last minute when Valerio, Mariana's pretended, arrives with documentation about Tartufo's past. The contrast between Tartufo's sanctimonious perfidy and Orgon's ingenuousness parallels the development of Molière's play. The striking differences found in the Cossa/Ardiles Gray version are the abbreviation of the text (from five acts to one), the change from verse to prose, the modernization of the language with a natural sound and context (although divorced from any specific time or location), and the surprise ending. While the original results in the king's intervention with Tartuffe going to prison, Cossa twists the final scene so that Tartufo is invited to remain in the house for a final banquet, a typical Cossa orgy of eating and drinking. The spirit of the original lies close beneath the surface of this play, one of Cossa's few works ostensibly disconnected from an Argentine reality. The metaphorical implications of artifice, hypocrisy, and greed transcend time and space, bedevil modern society, and leave trails of human suffering in their wake, wherever they occur.

Two plays postdate the four published volumes. One is *Lejos de aquí* (Far from here, 1993), Cossa's second play written in collaboration, this one with Mauricio Kartun. With resonances of *Gris de ausencia*, the play is set outside Madrid in a small restaurant called Pampas Argentinas where the five characters exercise their fantasies of living in some other time, past or present, and some other place where life was/is/will be better. As usual, Cossa develops credible characters with interesting histories in which all are malcontents, seeking happiness through their illusions of utopias to be found in other places. As with some previous plays, this one deals with nationality differences as well, as the restaurant serves as a cross-cultural microcosm (Argentine, Colombian, Galician, German, etc.). The basic feeling is one of frustration, a *mal de siècle*, a sense of not belonging to anybody, coupled with desperate efforts to identify with conditions that will bring instantaneous happiness.

Cossa's most recent play, as of this writing, is *Viejos conocidos* (Old acquaintances, 1994), the dramatization of two old friends who meet by coincidence on the train. The train provides a venue, as in *El sur y después*, for uncovering the past, for penetrating the psyche to find hidden meanings. As with Cossa's other plays, this one is also a work of political protest but couched in a new language. With a style bordering on the surrealistic at times, the language is rapid, virtually telegraphic. As the two reminisce, it becomes clear that one of them has a limited memory for names, the other a limited memory for faces. The recurrent motif, the touchstone of the play, is the protest against the *latifundistas* [landowners] whose controlling interests skewed the economic and political process in Argentina from the time of President Rivadavia onward. Some of the characters change identities; a young girl on a bicycle occasionally rides by, nude, as a past vision of better times, but the memory and image turn to that of an old woman, signifying disillusion with present conditions. The play stands as an enduring testimony to Cossa's inventiveness in finding new formulas for interpreting the past as measured against present realities.

In conclusion, the net impact of twenty plays written over exactly thirty years (1964–1994) indicates that Roberto Cossa is not only one of the most substantial playwrights of Argentina but also of the Latin American world. His plays are pithy and effective, communicating a strong message of the social, political, economic, and cultural conditions of their times. It is worthy of note that as Cossa advances in age (from thirty to sixty), his characters also tend to grow older, if not wiser. Throughout the years, however, there are certain constants in his work that bear repeating. One is the proclivity toward short, one-act plays, whose running time is usually an hour to ninety minutes. This length does not allow much time for character development, which presupposes that in most cases his characters will belong to certain types or classes. Many times, in fact, they carry designations such as El Viejo, La Madre, and Nuera.

The second most fundamental characteristic is Cossa's commitment to sociopolitical conditions in his country and the manner in which he tracks their development over the years. Although his own political inclinations lie considerably to the left, the plays focus not so much on advocacy as on results, leaving the reader/spectator with the undeniable impression that his characters are incapable of creating a system of governance that serves the general good because of their hypocrisy, corruption, and attention to self-interests. They exemplify greed and opportunism that work to the detriment of the society at large, and, therefore, to the individuals themselves. For the most part, all these attributes are couched within realistic frameworks with occasional time/space diversions. Humor, especially black humor, is another constant. In the fine tradition of the Argentine grotesque, Cossa manipulates both linguistic and situational humor to provide entertaining diversions while delivering to his audience/reader a concept of deteriorating conditions. With the native heritage of Armando Discépolo and Enrique Santos Discépolo, tempered by the social and ethical realism of Arthur Miller, Cossa is a master at interpreting the ambiance that he knows best, that is, the *porteño* lifestyle of the middle class, with its music, especially the classical strains of the Argentine tango. His plays derive from, and often depend on, musical motifs as well as the social milieu of eating and drinking, especially to excess. The sense of nostalgia that pervades his plays leaves the reader/audience with a sad reflection over what Argentina could be, were it to achieve its potential. Without wanting to "cry for me, Argentina," one is nonetheless moved to compassion for a people deprived of an essential part of a rich heritage.

Notes

1. Susana Poujol, "*Yepeto*: Una poética de la escritura," *Espacio de Crítica e Investigación* 1, no. 4 (1988): 51.

2. For further biographical detail, see Donald Yates's introduction to *Nuestro fin de semana* (New York: Macmillan, 1966).

3. Ibid., 4.

4. Luis Ordaz, "Prólogo," Carlos Gorostiza, *Los hermanos queridos*; Roberto Cossa, *La nona* (Buenos Aires: Sociedad General de Autores de la Argentina, 1980), 10.

5. Osvaldo Pellettieri, *La pata de la sota. Ya nadie recuerda a Frederic Chopin* (Buenos Aires: Clásicos Huemul, 1985), 24.

6. Roberto Cossa, *Teatro* (Buenos Aires: Ediciones de la Flor, 1987–1991). Vol. 1, 1987: *Nuestro fin de semana. Los días de Julián Bisbal. La ñata contra el libro. La pata de la sota. Tute cabrero.* Vol. 2, 1989: *El avión negro. La nona. No hay que llorar.* Vol. 3, 1990: *El viejo criado. Gris de ausencia. Ya nadie recuerda a Frederic Chopin. De pies y manos. Yepeto. El sur y después.* Vol. 4, 1991: *Angelito. Los compadritos. Tartufo* (adaptación). Quotations from Cossa's plays are from this edition and are cited in the text by volume and page numbers. Translations are mine.

7. See Cossa, *Teatro*, 2:8.

8. For more detail, see George Woodyard, "Towards a Radical Theatre in Spanish America," in *Contemporary Latin American Literature,* ed. Harvey L. Johnson and Phillip B. Taylor, Jr. (Houston: University of Houston Press, 1973), 93–102.

9. See Cossa, *Teatro*, 2:8.

10. The coincidence of the two dates led Cossa to write to a high school newspaper on the subject, for which he was severely reprimanded during the Peronista period.

Metatheatre and Parody in the Generation of 1924: The Cases of Arlt and Villaurrutia

Peter Roster
Carleton University

CRITICISM on the avante-garde in Latin America has focused mainly on poetry, and, to a lesser degree, on the narrative; but not much attention has been given to the corresponding movement in theatre. Nevertheless, it existed; and it produced some excellent plays that, unfortunately, have generally been overlooked or relegated to positions of secondary importance. This study will focus on two plays that were written and staged during that period. My interest was drawn to the topic in the course of preparing a longer study on the generational method. One of the undeniable values of this approach is its ability to call attention to similarities between writers that might otherwise have escaped notice. This is precisely what happened in the case of the present study, and for that reason it constitutes the backdrop for the rest of this discussion.

The complete works of Xavier Villaurrutia and Roberto Arlt have both received considerable critical notice; but in both cases, neither *Parece mentira* (Incredible) nor *El fabricante de fantasmas* (The maker of dreams) have been the recipients of much more than scant praise. In the case of Villaurrutia, more heed has been paid to the longer plays and to his poetry. In the case of Arlt, more criticism has focused on his participation in the Teatro del Pueblo and his role in a socially oriented theatre; but again, scant consideration has been given to his one abortive incursion into the commercial theatre: the production of *El fabricante de fantasmas* in 1936. A close reading of both works will show that, in effect, they are innovative plays that exemplify some of the first and most profound examples of what has since come to be known as metatheatre. It is not at all strange that the plays were a commercial flop since both Arlt and Villaurrutia were in fact parodying the dominant dramatic system of that period, including the very audience for which they were staged. Seen in this light, they represent some of the first examples of Latin American theatrical modernism, and, at times, they border on what we would now call a postmodern tone.

The Generation of 1924 (according to José Juan Arrom's divisions),[1] or of 1927 (according to Cedomil Goič),[2] is the generation of the avant-garde, responsible for having wrought some of the most radical changes in Spanish American literature of this century. It was an iconoclastic generation whose members were born, approximately, between 1890 and 1909, appeared on the literary scene around 1920, and reached their literary maturity during the period from 1924 to 1953. Among its members were some of the most distinguished names in Spanish American letters: Vicente Huidobro, César Vallejo, Nicolás Guillén, and Pablo Neruda in poetry; Roberto Arlt, Jorge Luis Borges, Alejo Carpentier, Eduardo Mallea, and Agustín Yáñez in fiction; and, representing theatre, dramatists like Roberto Arlt and Xavier Villaurrutia.

The intragenerational conflict[3] centers around the universal/nationalistic split, and between the autonomous nature of the work of art as opposed to its utility as a vehicle of social change. This is the conflict that, in rather simplistic terms, is symbolized by literary groups of opposing ideological positions, such as Boedo and Florida in Argentina and Contemporáneos and Estridentistas in Mexico. In general, it is more acute during the first generational phase. Over time, the respective initial stances tend to become less rigid, and the authors frequently borrow techniques from the previously antagonistic group, with the result that the works ultimately wind up as a blend of both. For example, there were authors who, like Salvador Novo in Mexico, started out writing or being identified as elitists only to end up creating works with a distinctly nationalistic flavor; on the other hand, there were writers initially classified as socially committed, like Mauricio Magdaleno and Juan Bustillo Oro, creators of the Teatro de Ahora (1932), who ironically wound up being technically innovative when they introduced expressionistic and other European techniques in their plays.[4]

Whereas, in poetry, the shocking image that relates elements drawn from the most disparate realms of experience stands out as the characteristic that defines the dominant style of the period, in prose, it is the use of a narrator who moves toward man's inner landscape and stations himself in the innermost spaces of his being that reveals itself as the most lasting literary legacy. And if, in the case of poetry, we can safely say that Vicente Huidobro's famous exhortation "No cantéis la rosa, poetas, hacedla florecer en el poema" [Don't sing of the rose, poets, make it bloom in the poem]—a principle that led him to produce such extraordinary images as "[Soy] una flor de contradicciones / bailando un fox-trot sobre el sepulcro de Dios" [(I am) a flower of contradictions / dancing a fox-trot on the grave of God][5]—became the prototypical banner under which the essence of these avant-garde renovations was presented, then, in the case of the theatre, we can equally well state that the transcendence of realism through the use of metatheatrical and parodic techniques became the most enduring and significant contribution made by the dramatists of this generation. As examples of this tendency, this study will concentrate on *Parece mentira* by the Mexican, Xavier Villaurrutia (1903), and *El fabricante de fantasmas* by the Argentine, Roberto Arlt (1900).

It was Arlt's works in prose fiction that first called attention to his literary talents, specifically the publication in 1926 of his short novel, *El juguete rabioso*, that stands out as one of the early examples of the psychological novel.[6] Only through the insistence of Leónidas Barletta, who, in 1931 in his Teatro del Pueblo, with the title of *El humillado*, created a stage version of a chapter of Arlt's novel, *Los siete locos*, did Arlt become interested in the theatre; and only in 1932 did he present his first work for the theatre, *Trescientos millones*. From that point until his death in 1942 he devoted himself almost exclusively to the theatre, leaving behind a total of about ten plays, some just recently published.

The Teatro del Pueblo and the Contribution of Leónidas Barletta

In the words of Raúl Larra, author of *Leónidas Barletta: El hombre de la campana*, "El ámbito teatral . . . se debatía en la decadencia más entristecedora. Salvo el acierto de algunos sainetes y la aparición de un autor original como Armando Discépolo . . . lo demás era chatura y bajo [The theatre scene . . . was in the midst of a most saddening decline. With the exception of a few *sainetes* and the arrival of a talented author like Armando Discépolo . . . it was all worse than mediocre and crass].[7]

Within this overall pessimistic theatre climate and shortly after the coup of 6 September 1930, which brought the dictator, General Uriburu, to power, Barletta managed to form the Teatro del Pueblo and stage his first work in 1931. During the official opening ceremony, he proposed "realizar experiencias de teatro moderno para salvar el envilecido arte teatral y llevar a las masas el arte en general, con el objeto de propender a la elevación espiritual de nuestro pueblo" [to carry out experiments in modern theatre in order to rescue the sullied image of the theatre and take art in general to the masses, thereby contributing to the spiritual edification of our people] (*LB*, 72).

Without going into the specifics contained in the articles of the constitution of the Teatro del Pueblo, their primary aim according to Luis Ordaz was to combat the three basic blights that plagued the theatre of that time: 1) the star system of prima donnas and leading actors; 2) the subservience of art to the profit motive; and 3) the absolute control exercised by the impresario who invariably converted the theatre into a money-oriented enterprise.[8] It was from the desire to rid themselves of this state of affairs that this type of small theatre group came to be called *free* or *independent* theatres.

Mexican Theatre in the 1920s

The state of the theatre in Mexico in the 1920s was not much different from the Argentine situation: an antiquated repertoire controlled by a small number of commercial companies whose impresarios were more interested in ticket sales than in the quality of the works or the development of a national theatre movement. Villaurrutia's interest in theatre was evident as early as 1927 when he co-founded the Teatro Ulises. The objectives of Ulises were fundamentally two: 1) to educate the public by offering them a selection of the best Spanish classic plays as well as translations of the best contemporary foreign works; and 2) to give the best Mexican authors the possibility of seeing their own works staged. The fact that this venture lasted a scant two years doesn't do justice to its effect on the Mexican theatrical scene, the fruit of which was seen in the establishment of other experimental groups, particularly Teatro Orientación, during the 1930s. Essentially, Ulises, Orientación, and other similar and even more ephemeral groups are the Mexican equivalent of the independent theatre movement in Buenos Aires.

Just as the Argentine groups of Boedo and Florida engaged in polemics among themselves due to their opposing ideas on ethical and aesthetic questions, and still continued to form part of the same generation, so also did the Contemporáneos and Estridentistas in Mexico represent different facets and constitute different groups of the same avant-garde generation, the Generation of 1924. Using these assertions as necessary background, this study proposes that the Mexican and Argentine generations of avant-garde represented by Villaurrutia's *Parece mentira* and Arlt's *El fabricante de fantasmas* partake of that spirit of serious curiosity and adventure that typifies the most important theatrical innovations of this century, and, more specifically, that a fundamental part of that renovation are the distinctive characteristics of the phenomenon that has come to be called self-conscious literature, or metaliterature.

Parody

From a slightly different perspective, these same techniques also function as examples of parody—understood in the sense of transformations that were indicative of transitions from one period to another and that were brought about by the recasting in unfamiliar ways of worn-out literary conventions. In these specific cases, what had been typical motifs of the bourgeois drama of the time continued to provide the initial situations of the works. However, rather than using them to provoke an easy laugh or superficial responses, they now served as a frame of reference that contained more profound levels of significance, much in the same manner that Borges used the detective story in "La muerte y la brújula" (Death and the compass) as a point of departure for his metaphysical speculations.

Metatheatre

While what we now refer to as metaliterary techniques and works have existed since at least the time of Cervantes, Shakespeare, and Calderón, it is only in the last thirty years, and more frequently during the last twenty, that they have come to constitute a significant term and tactic, of special interest to both critics and writers. With specific reference to the theatre, it was Lionel Abel who, in 1963, in a collection of articles published under the title of *Metatheatre: A New View of Dramatic Form,*[9] seems to have been the first to use the term in a precise fashion. Since then, articles and book-length studies have proliferated, not only with respect to the theatre, but also and especially about prose fiction: Alter, Barth,

Dotras, Hornby, Hutcheon, Rose, Schlueter, and Waugh, among others;[10] and, in Hispanic criticism, Foster, Kronik, Meléndez, Spires, and Dotras in 1994,[11] to give just a partial list. While the nomenclature and perspectives invariably differ, we are now at a point where we can confidently delineate the basic characteristics, forms, and principles of metatheatre.

The most common techniques are:

1) The use of a play-within-a-play: Shakespeare in *Hamlet*; Pirandello in *Enrico IV*; Victor Manuel Díez Barroso in *Véncete a ti mismo.*

2) Role-within-a-role, when one character plays a second role within his initial one: Enrico IV, Saverio in Arlt's *Saverio el cruel*; the two sisters in Genet's *Las criadas.*

3) The use of literary allusions, allusions to the contemporary, real world, many times in the form of traditional parody: *Antígona furiosa* by Griselda Gambaro.

4) The use of contradictory or incompatible situations or endings: short stories of Borges, "La muerte y la brújula" and "Biblioteca de Babel," or the film *High Heels* by Almodóvar.

5) Reference to theatrical conventions and the creative process: *La señorita de Tacna* by Mario Vargas Llosa; *Historias para ser contadas* by Osvaldo Dragún.

6) The presence of a self-referring character capable of dramatizing other characters, thereby creating a second level of theatricality or fiction: Saverio in *Saverio el cruel.*

All of these techniques invariably involve making the artifice overt. They make use of the vocabulary commonly related to the creative process and have the common objective of calling attention to themselves, to the work as a fiction, as an alternate reality or as a fabricated reality. All of this is contrary to the mimetic concept of art as a reflection of reality, which has served as the model of Western theatrical tradition. In essence, culture replaces nature as the subject of art. The outside world of supposed every-day reality ceases to be the referent of the theatrical sign. In its place are theatrical tradition, theatrical creation, theatrical reality, and the creative process itself. That is to say that structure, situation, dialogue, and language itself acquire significance only within their relation to elements of the drama/culture complex[12] to which they belong. In other words, those elements create and acquire their meaning by means of a system of literary and fictional intrareferences, and not by referring to what is considered daily and palpable reality.

These techniques force the reader/spectator to reflect on the nature and process of the creative act and on the relation between everyday reality and the reality of the theatrical world. They also have the effect of making the spectator uncomfortable because they contradict the normal expectations of traditional theatre as a reflection of exterior reality. As a consequence, a double and ambiguous vision of reality is created in the spectator. Instead of having meaning, solutions, and conclusions provided, the spectator is left with doubts and is forced to construct a personal conclusion. We can say, then, that metatheatre aims to do away with the normal transparency with which one customarily receives and interprets theatre. It achieves this by making its own codes, conventions, and artifices seem apparent and visible, and thereby converting them into the object of their own actions.

Metatheatrical Elements in *Parece mentira*

In the specific case of Villaurrutia, it is clear that he felt the need to participate in the renovation of a theatre that, in his own words, was characterized by "sucios locales, viejos actores, anacrónicas decoraciones e imposibles repertorios [y en el que] la vejez parece ser su atmósfera necesaria; la improvisación, su único método; la incultura, su contenido. Vejez, improvisación e incultura se alían para encerrar al teatro en un oscuro e irrespirable recinto" [rundown theatres, aging actors, anachronistic decorations and impossible repertoires (and in which) old age seems to be the indispensable atmosphere; improvisation, the only method; poor taste, its content. Old age, improvisation, and poor taste join forces to lock the theatre into a dingy, stifling chamber.[13]

Presented with the opening scene of *Parece mentira* (two people in the waiting room of a lawyer's office: one not knowing why he's there; and the other, the Marido [Husband] who has received an anonymous letter saying that he would find his currently unfaithful wife there), the audience is prepared to witness the unfolding of a typical melodrama; but Villaurrutia's denouement frustrates that expectation. What is achieved with that resolution, then, is a nonfulfillment of the horizon of expectations: the author toys with the audience at the same time that he is subverting the traditional form of the bourgeois drama. In other words, the superficially humorous function typical of the love-triangle plot has been given new life and more intellectual substance through the reformulation of a plot that now questions and even undermines traditional ideas regarding the nature of theatre, human personality, the nature of reality, and the relation between reality and theatre.

All of this is *curious* but not at all surprising if we compare the effect achieved by Villaurrutia in this work with the author's own statements on theatre:

> La imitación servil, fotográfica, de los modelos exteriores y de los fragmentos de vida también exterior, han venido relegando al teatro a un lugar que no merece entre todas las artes.
> El autor dramático olvida, las más de las veces, que es un inventor, un creador, un poeta; y que la obra de teatro tiene el deber de objetivar y materializar, no aquello que de hecho ya está objetivado y materializado a los ojos de todos, sino aquello que aún no lo está y que, profundo y huidizo, merece estarlo.

> [The servile, photographic imitation of exterior models and of slices of life, also external, have come to relegate theatre to an undeserved place among the arts.
> The dramatic author forgets, most of the time, that he is an inventor, a creator, a poet; and that a theatrical work has an obligation to objectify and to materialize, not what is already in fact objectified and visible in everyone's eyes, but rather to make visible what is still invisible and which, because of its profound and elusive nature, deserves to be made visible.][14]

In addition to what has just been pointed out, Villaurrutia managed to give new functions to other traditional elements that he considered clichéd and unimaginative, particularly, language, characters, the ending, and the subject matter itself.

With respect to language, right from the start of the play, and especially beginning with the second scene, there is a series of plays on words that, in this work, even accepting that they are typical of the bourgeois drama, set the stage for the metaphysical enigma that is presented at the end. On the other hand, in and of themselves, they are concrete examples of that overall theme since they show how deceptive and ambiguous language, as one of the elements of reality, really is, and how words, as signs, conceal behind the same physical representation, behind their unique graphical image, multiple facets, multiple and contradictory meanings, even while they simultaneously continue pointing to all of them.

Two short examples will suffice to clarify this statement:

El Curioso. ¿El señor Fernández es joven?
. . . .

El Empleado. Comparado con el señor padre del señor Fernández, el señor Fernández es joven; comparado con el hijo del señor Fernández, el señor Fernández ya no es joven.

[*Curious Man.* Is Mr. Fernández a young man?
. . . .
Employee. Compared to Mr. Fernández's father, Mr. Fernández is young; compared with Mr. Fernández's son, Mr. Fernández is no longer young.][15]

And later on:

El Curioso. No hay duda, es usted el perfecto secretario particular.
El Empleado. No soy el secretario particular del abogado. . . . El señor Fernández no tiene secretos. ¿Por qué había de tener secretario? . . . Soy un simple empleado.

[*Curious Man.* Without a doubt, you are the perfect private secretary.
Employee. But I'm not the advocate's private secretary. . . . Mr. Fernández doesn't have any secrets, so why would he have a secretary? . . . I'm just an employee, pure and simple.]

(*PM*, 99)

Just as the written word cannot be univocal, neither can the essence of a man be considered unifacetic. As Pirandello stated in his essay on humor:

And precisely the various tendencies that mark the personality lead us seriously to think that the individual soul is not *one*. How can we claim that it is *one*, in fact, if passion and reason, instinct and will, tendencies and ideals constitute as many separate and mobile systems functioning in such a way that the individual—living now one of them, now another, and now some compromise between two or more psychic tendencies—appears as if he really has within himself several different and even opposed souls, several different and conflicting personalities?[16]

Pirandello's idea is echoed in the Empleado's assertion that "en cada uno de nosotros existen simultáneamente, sentimientos contradictorios hacia una misma cosa, hacia una misma persona" [there exist simultaneously in each of us contradictory feelings about the same thing, about the same person] (*PM*, 100).

As far as characters are concerned, El Curioso and El Marido represent two contradictory personality types; even more, we would say that, in addition to constituting the basic dramatic conflict, they personify—as well as two ways of understanding and creating art (the unifacetic, mimetic realistic way, and the polyfacetic, antimimetic and metadramatic way)—the two types of *curiosity* described by Villaurrutia in his essay on the work of Sor Juana Inés de la Cruz. In that essay, he distinguished between a masculine- and a femenine-type curiosity. Feminine-type curiosity is characterized as superficial, like El Curioso's:

> Yo distingo dos clases de curiosidad: la curiosidad de tipo masculino y la curiosidad de tipo femenino. Un hombre puede tener curiosidad femenina y una mujer curiosidad masculina. Este es el caso de Sor Juana.
>
> La curiosidad como una pasión que no acrecienta el poder del espíritu la podemos personificar en Eva, que mordió por curiosidad el fruto prohibido. En Pandora, que movida también por ese pensamiento abrió la caja que la habían prohibido. Esta es una curiosidad de tipo accidental; pero hay otro tipo de curiosidad, una curiosidad más seria, más profunda, que es un producto del espíritu y que también es una fuente en el conocimiento. Esta curiosidad como pasión, no como capricho—la curiosidad de Pandora es un capricho—, es la curiosidad de Sor Juana.
>
> ¿Qué es curiosidad por pasión? Yo la defino así: es una especie de avidez del espíritu y de los sentidos que deteriora el gusto del presente en provecho de la aventura; es una especie de riesgo que se hace más agudo a medida que el confort en que se vive es más largo. . . . Como ejemplo puedo dar a ustedes un personaje . . . Simbad el Marino [quien] dueño de riquezas, no se conforma con su comodidad, con su holgura [sino que] rico y pobre en su riqueza, en cuanto el tedio lo amenaza abandona riquezas y bienes y se lanza a la aventura.

[I distinguish between two types of curiosity: a masculine and a feminine type. A man can have a feminine kind of curiosity just as a woman can have a masculine kind. This is Sor Juana's case.

Curiosity as a passion that doesn't increase spiritual power is personified by Eve, who was moved by curiosity to take a bite of the forbidden fruit. And also by Pandora, who was moved by that same thought to open the box in spite of the fact that it was prohibited. This is an accidental type of curiosity; but there is a different kind, more serious, more profound, that is a product of the spirit and also a source of knowledge. This type of curiosity as a passion, not a whim— Pandora's curiosity is a whim—is Sor Juana's type of curiosity.

What constitutes curiosity as a passion? I define it as follows: it is a type of eagerness that encompasses both the spirit and the senses, and that sacrifices immediate pleasure in favor of adventure; it's a feeling of risk that becomes sharper even as the level of comfort in which one lives becomes more pervasive. . . . As an example, I can suggest a character . . . Sinbad the Sailor (who), possessed of riches, was not content with his comfort, with his comfortable life (but rather) both rich and poor in his wealth, as soon as boredom approached him, abandoned his wealth and his riches and set off on his adventure.][17]

Like Sinbad, at the end of *Parece mentira,* El Marido launches himself on the adventurous path of self-knowledge and thereby rejects the easier road of security chosen by El Curioso, who will continue to wear the same fixed and unchanging mask of comfort.

What we have then, in place of the typical ending that might have been a separation, a reconciliation, or some act of violence, is a scene (repeated three times) that changes the whole character of the work: the three separate arrivals of a veiled woman are seen from three distinct perspectives. For El Curioso, three different women come in, and from that point until his exit from stage he can only make sense of this event by repeating the question, "Which of the three?," since his understanding of the world is incapable of accepting any deeper alternative. On the other hand, El Marido undergoes three distinct reactions that represent different facets of his personality. El Empleado finds just one business card in his pocket, and for the first time in the play, he offers no reply, thereby leaving the solution of the enigma to the spectator/reader.

In keeping with this idea, the Abogado finally arrives, sees off El Marido, and the play ends without having offered any definitive conclusion about how to interpret this incident that, instead of being a slice of life with a corresponding realistic thesis, leaves us with the several seemingly incompatible and irreconcilable versions.

Over the extremely short and only act of this play, El Empleado rids himself of his initial mold and metamorphoses into a true metacharacter, who, aware of his multiple condition of actor/character/dramatist, dramatizes the other characters. In one of the initial dialogues, El Curioso points out what was already apparent in the ingenious replies of El Empleado: he is truly an employee who sounds more like a poet. Starting from that observation, the frame of reference and interpretation is necessarily broadened to include the creative process; with that, we enter into a double-visioned realm. The convention of dramatic illusion that existed during the opening scene is broken, and the spectator/reader needs to put on his bifocals in order to adapt to the subsequent events.

In later speeches, the Empleado-Poeta discourses·directly on the relation between author, reality, character, and audience:

El Empleado. En mí se dan la mano el empleado y el poeta, pero lo más frecuente es la ignorancia de estos dobleces de la personalidad.

[*Employee.* In me, the employee and the poet are joined; but in most cases these quirks of personality go unnoticed.]

(*PM*, 100)

And:

El Empleado. Si no se atreve a hablar y pensando que necesita hacerlo ... yo podría interpetar sus sentimientos con las mismas palabras con que usted hablaría. Tengo esa costumbre. Desde pequeño confesaba los pecados cometidos por los demás. Tengo el dón, el secreto o la habilidad, a veces muy dolorosos, de hacer hablar a las cosas y a los seres. De sus palabras, hago mis poesías; de sus confesiones, mis novelas. . . . No me diga nada. Yo imagino su caso y siento lo que imagino.

[*Employee.* If you are afraid to speak and still thinking that you need to do so . . . I could interpret your feelings with the very words that you would use. I'm accustomed to it. Even as a child I used to confess to sins committed by others. I have the gift, key or ability, at times rather painful, to make things and beings speak. From their words, I create my poems; from their confessions, my novels. . . . Don't say a word. I can imagine your case and I feel (for) what I imagine.

(*PM*, 106)

Scarcely have these words been uttered/read when we realize that this play is a dramatization of the theory. In fact, we are witnessing a subversion of traditional theatre at the same time as the creation of an innovative work that—without, obviously, eliminating all references to the recognizable, familiar objects of daily life—begins to dialogue with and about itself.

Metatheatrical Elements in *El fabricante de fantasmas*

As is the case in the majority of Arlt's plays, the story is simple: Pedro, a young married dramatist finds himself in matrimonial difficulty because his wife, Eloísa, has decided to withhold conjugal delights until he finds a job. Faced with this problem, he is suddenly tempted to solve the problem by entering into an extramarital relationship with Martina, a friend of his wife's. To this point, we have nothing more than the promise of a variation on the shopworn amorous-triangle plot. Then, in an abrupt change of course that Arlt called an impromptu, Pedro is presented with an opportunity to resolve his problem in a totally different fashion: by doing away with his wife. This is the course he chooses as he pushes her out of a window. Later, after being exonerated from all blame in the accidental death of his wife, he marries Martina, continues with his writing career and becomes extremely successful. The action continues in this vein until the premiere of a work in which he presents the case of a dramatist who kills his wife and eludes punishment. On the level of the first frame, the judge who originally acquitted Pedro pays him a visit and speaks to him about the play and the inevitable psychological repercussions it must have on him. Troubled now, Pedro takes a trip to rid himself of the memory. In a carnival scene, either real or imagined, he finds himself with a costumed figure who looks exactly like his dead wife. He returns home in a weakened, feverish state, where, in a hallucinatory scene, his feelings of remorse appear in human form as a humpback, a prostitute, and a cripple who together are charged with the task of forcing him to commit suicide in the same way that he killed his wife, that is, by throwing himself out a window.

In order to relate these actions to a metatheatrical interpretation, we need to mention certain elements of Arlt's thinking on the nature and purpose of theatre in general, and, specifically, his attitude toward the theatre in Buenos Aires of the 1930s. Clearly, he drew a line between the commercial theatre and the free or independent theatre movement. He pointed out that "mientras que la obra del autor comercial maniene su clima en absoluta conexión con un público y un actor previamente clasificados, la obra del autor independiente hace abstracción de estos elementos. La obra del autor independiente es un suceso personal. Acaecido a él y para él" [while the work of an author in the commercial theatre maintains an atmosphere that is in total agreement with a public and a type of actor that are totally known to him, the author of experimental plays makes an abstraction of those elements. The work of the experimental playwright is a personal event—one that has happened to him and for him] (LB, 76).

In certain key passages of the *Fabricante*, the protagonist, Pedro, talks about dramatic art, and, according to people who knew Arlt personally, they are accurate reflections of the author's ideas. Just like the speech of the Secretario of *Parece mentira,* they open the door to a discussion of the creative process:

> Para mí, el teatro es un medio de plantearle problemas personales a la humanidad ... En este caso mis problemas. Necesito urgentemente subir a un escenario y decirle a un público cuya cara sea invisible en la oscuridad: "Me pasa esto, aquello, lo otro. ¿Cómo resuelvo los enigmas que bailan en mi conciencia?" Ya ve, los otros quieren llegar al escenario para darle satisfacción a un problema, a su vanidad ... Yo no ... es un problema personal ... auténticamente personal.

> [As far as I'm concerned, theatre is a way of presenting personal problems to mankind ... In this case, my own problems. I urgently need to get up on a stage and say to an audience whose face is invisible in the darkness: "This, that, and the next thing, that's what's bothering me. How can I resolve the enigmas that are dancing around in my head?" So you see, the others (dramatists) want the stage to satisfy only one need, their vanity ... Not in my case ... it's a personal problem ... authentically personal.[18]

The comments of Pedro-Dramatist concerning the public are important since they help to further solidify the bases for the metatheatrical interpretation:

> La gente que acude a los teatros va en busca de lo que no existe en sus vidas. Podría decirse que las mentiras son para ellos las puertas de oro que se abren a un país encantado. Nosotros, autores, no nos podemos formar ni la más remota idea acerca de la arbitraria estructura de aquellos países de ensueño, en los que se mueve la imaginación del público. Como los alquimistas jugamos con fuerzas naturales cuyos efectos parecen mágicos, pues unas veces la muchedumbre aplaude y otras bosteza.

> [The people who go to the theatre are looking for something that doesn't exist in their own lives. You might say that, for them, lies are like golden doors that open onto an enchanted place. We, the authors, can't allow ourselves to form even the vaguest notion of the arbitrary structure of those enchanted worlds of the public's imagination. Rather like alchemists we play with natural forces whose effects seem magical, since some times the crowds applaud and at others they simply yawn.]

(*FF,* 126)

Among Arlt's thoughts on theatre, there are many that one automatically associates with Pirandello: the idea of the independence of the theatrical character that in Arlt is linked at the same time with the idea of theatre as an externalization of personal conflicts:

> Lucha cruel. El fantasma es tan rebelde como el ser humano que representa. . . . ¿Te das cuenta? Para muchos hombres, cortos de imaginación, únicamente pueden existir conflictos teatrales entre cuerpos de carne y hueso . . . ¡Qué ciegos! Todavía no han comprendido que el hombre de carne y hueso es sobre la tierra un fantasma tan vano como la sombra que se mueve en la pared.

> [Cruel struggle. A ghost is just as rebellious as the character he represents. . . . Don't you see that for many people, lacking imagination, theatrical conflicts can only exist between flesh-and-blood people . . . How blind can they be! They still haven't realized that the flesh-and-blood human that walks the earth is as much a ghost as the shadow on a wall.]

> (*FF*, 128)

El fabricante de fantasmas is, then, a basically metatheatrical work in which the protagonist is a dramatist *in the process of writing* who sees passing before him the different possible ways of *playing a scene*. This corresponds, first of all, to the Teatro del Pueblo and the way in which Arlt actually worked with the actors. In the second place, it relates to the plot of this play and the interpretation of the death of his wife as just *one of the possible endings that Arlt-author could have given to this play*. Consequently, each possibility rejected is, from the point of view of the creative process, a death for which the author is responsible and for which he feels personally to blame and full of remorse.

The play functions, then, on various levels simultaneously: on one level, Pedro-Man struggles with his conscience for actually having killed his wife; on another level, Pedro-Author, and by extension, Arlt-Dramatist, struggles with the ghosts of all the characters who might have had a life, or at least a different and less anguished one, had he not killed them off or had he changed their dramatic role.

Conclusion

Both Villaurrutia and Arlt were innovators in the theatre movements of their respective countries. They availed themselves of familiar, "exhausted"[19] situations typical of the realistic theatre of the period only in order to give them a different twist and thereby transform them into metatheatrical works that establish a dialogue with and about the process of artistic creation. In doing this, they managed to give added depth to their works and to revitalize and "replenish"[20] the theatre of their time. As well, their innovative techniques placed them in the vanguard of modernist theatrical renovation, which is, after all, the artistic legacy of the Generation of 1924 in Latin America.

Notes

1. José Juan Arrom, *Esquema generacional de las letras hispanoamericanas: Esbozo de un método*, 2d ed. (Bogota: Instituto Caro y Cuervo, 1977).

2. Cedomil Goič, *Historia de la novela hispanoamericana* (Valparaiso: Ediciones Universitarias de Valparaíso, 1972).

3. For a more detailed discussion of this topic, see Peter Roster, "Generational Transition in Argentina: From Fray Mocho to Teatro Abierto (1956–1985)," *Latin American Theatre Review* 25, no. 1 (Fall 1991): 21–40.

4. Frank Dauster, *Perfil generacional del teatro hispanoamericano (1894–1954): Chile, México, El Río de la Plata* (Ottawa: Girol, 1993), 170.

5. This and all translations, unless otherwise noted, are mine.

6. What I am referring to here is what Goič calls the "novela de conciencia"; other examples would be Mallea's *Fiesta en noviembre* and María Luisa Bombal's *La última niebla*. The point is to contrast the location of the narrator (internal, from the perspective of feelings and thoughts), as opposed to the until-then-dominant external third-person narrator. Later, it develops into the stream of consciousness, but that is still twenty years away as far as the development of the Latin American novel is concerned.

7. Raúl Larra, *Leónidas Barletta: El hombre de la campana* (Buenos Aires: Ediciones Conducta, 1978), 71. Hereafter *LB*, cited in text.

8. Luis Ordaz, *Aproximación a la trayectoria de la dramática argentina* (Ottawa: Girol, 1992), 48.

9. Lionel Abel, *Metatheatre: A New View of Dramatic Form* (New York: Hill & Wang, 1963).

10. Robert Alter, *Partial Magic:The Novel as a Self-Conscious Genre* (Berkeley: University of California Press, 1975); Richard Hornby, *Drama, Metadrama, and Perception* (Lewisburg, Pa.: Bucknell University Press, 1986); Linda Hutcheon, *Narcissistic Narrative: The Metafictional Paradox*, 2d ed. (New York: Methuen, 1984); Margaret Rose, *Parody/Meta-fiction: An Analysis of Parody as a Critical Mirror to the Writing and Reception of Fiction* (London: Croom Helm, 1979); June Schlueter, *Metafictional Characters in Modern Drama* (New York: Columbia University Press, 1979); Patricia Waugh, *Metafiction: The Theory and Practice of Self-Conscious Fiction* (New York: Methuen, 1984).

11. David William Foster, "*Yo también hablo de la rosa* de Emilio Carballido: Los límites del teatro brechtiano," in *Estudios sobre teatro mexicano* (New York: Peter Lang, 1984); John W. Kronik, "*El gesticulador* and the Fiction of Truth," *Latin American Theatre Review* 11, no. 1 (1977): 5–16; Patricia Meléndez, *La dramaturgia hispanoamericana contemporánea: Teatralidad y autoconciencia* (Madrid: Pliegos, 1990); Robert Spires, *Beyond the Metafictional Mode: Directions in the Modern Spanish Novel* (Lexington: The University Press of Kentucky, 1984); Ana M. Dotras, *La novela española de metaficción* (Madrid: Júcar, 1994).

12. See Hornby, *Drama, Metadrama, and Perception*, 22.

13. Xavier Villaurrutia, "El teatro es así," in *Obras*, 2d ed., rev. (Mexico: Fondo de Cultura Económica, 1966), 736.

14. Xavier Villaurrutia, "El teatro. Recuerdos y figuras," *Revista de Bellas Artes*, quoted in Frank Dauster, *Xavier Villaurrutia* (New York: Twayne, 1971), 139.

15. Xavier Villaurrutia, *Parece mentira*, in *Obras*, 98, 99. Hereafter *PM*, cited in the text, with reference numbers referring to page numbers in *Obras*.

16. Luigi Pirandello, *On Humor*, trans. Antonio Illiano and Daniel P. Testa (Chapel Hill: University of North Carolina Studies in Comparative Literature, 1974), 136.

17. Xavier Villaurrutia, "Sor Juana Inés de la Cruz," *Obras*, 775–76.

18. Roberto Arlt, *El fabricante de fantasmas*, in *Teatro completo*, vol. 1 (Buenos Aires: Schapire, 1968), 75. Hereafter *FF*, cited in the text, with reference numbers referring to page numbers in *Teatro completo*. All quotations are from this edition.

19. John Barth, "The Literature of Exhaustion," *The Atlantic*, August 1967, 29–34.

20. John Barth, "The Literature of Replenishment," *The Atlantic*, August 1980, 65–71.

Comedy Revisited:
From *Rosalba y los Llaveros* to *Rosa de dos aromas*

Jacqueline Eyring Bixler
Virginia Polytechnic Institute and State University

E MILIO Carballido is without a doubt the best known, most prolific, and most commercially successful of Mexico's contemporary *comediógrafos*. Although he has experimented with a wide range of dramatic styles and genres, he first gained the spotlight of Mexican theatre with provincial, realist comedies, such as *Rosalba y los Llaveros* (Rosalba and the Llavero family, 1950) and *La danza que sueña la tortuga* (The dance the tortoise dreams, 1954).[1] *Rosalba* launched not only the 1950 theatre season for the Instituto Nacional de Bellas Artes and the dramatic career of its fledgling author, but also what Frank Dauster identifies as a new epoch for Mexican theatre: "One could say that [*Rosalba*] marks an epoch; after sentimental realism and professional comedy, which were either mediocre or not very Mexican, Carballido's theatre was a breath of fresh air. It showed the comic possibilities of provincial theatre, which until then was exclusively realist and costumbristic."[2] The fresh air that Carballido brought to the moribund Mexican theatre is the same one that accompanied Rosalba as she breezed into the stuffy and repressed household of her provincial relatives. To the solid but stodgy realism that dominated the Mexican stage during the 1940s and 1950s, Carballido added a distinctly Mexican language, a liberal dose of humor, and a twist of irony. Although these early comedies have not received nearly as much critical attention as other, more "complex" pieces, such as *Yo también hablo de la rosa* (I, too, speak of the rose) and *El diá que se soltaron los leones* (The day the lions got loose), they deserve further recognition as solid examples of modern comedy and as the foundation for much of Carballido's later theatre.

Three decades after the astounding success of *Rosalba* and after dabbling with a number of other dramatic genres, Carballido returns to comedy with *Rosa de dos aromas* (A rose by any other names, 1986), wherein he condenses the structure, cast, and dialogue of his early realistic comedies and revisits the question of liberation from a distinctly feminist angle.[3] The incredible commercial success of *Rosa,* his longest-running play, suggests that neither Carballido's comedies nor comedy in general have gone out of style. In fact, the recent re-premiere of *Rosalba y los Llaveros* suggests just the opposite.[4] The present study compares Carballido's first attempt at comedy and his latest box-office hit in an effort not only to recognize his ongoing efforts in this particular genre but also to move toward a definition of a genre that tends to be disregarded if not scorned by theorists as well as playwrights.[5]

Rosalba y los Llaveros offers a perfect point of departure in the exploration of Carballido's comedies, for it was not only his first comedy but also, as Dauster points out, "comedy in the strictest sense."[6] The only problem is, what exactly is a comedy? It is clearly more than just a happy ending and an irreflexive source of amusement, yet while Aristotle set the standards for the tragedies of his day as well as for all those to follow, there is no time-honored *Poetics* for comedy. One reason for the relative neglect of comedy is that critics and theorists tend to associate it with a lack of substance, aesthetic value, and originality. Another factor that has hindered efforts to define comedy is that these attempts inevitably lead to the even thornier question of laughter. Despite efforts by Bergson, Freud, and others to explain the phenomenon of laughter, no one can ever be sure of its causes or its function. Suzanne Langer, for example, acknowledges this problem when she asserts that the cause of laughter lies not in the object of the laughter but in the individual laugher.[7] Consequently, theorists like James Calderwood and Harold Toliver caution the reader against trying to define any genre by its elusive effects upon the receiver and instead urge the receiver to consider comedy's more "objective properties," such as structure, theme, style, and characterization.[8]

Following this reasoning, we first turn to the characters of comedy, most of whom exist somewhere between the puppetlike, stock types of farce and the complex heroes of tragedy. What Aristotle once disparagingly described as the "ignoble" are, in Wylie Sypher's more modern terms, "odd, lovable creatures" that secure a place in our hearts and our memory.[9] The main players tend to divide into what Harry Levin terms "playboys" and "killjoys": "Our proponent is pitted against an opponent seeking to constrict his freedom of action or to spoil his fun and games."[10] Curiously, in most Carballido comedies the playboy is a play*girl*, while the killjoy ranges from a whole house full of reticent relatives in *Rosalba* to the offstage patriarchal network of *Rosa*. Although Carballido provides a compassionate portrayal of women throughout his theatre, it is in his comedies where they most clearly get the upper hand in the everlasting battle between the sexes.

Today's comic hero is, according to Sypher, not just the average guy, but "the rebel, the immoralist, the free and licensed self [who] dares *play* with life."[11] In his/her struggle against the status quo, this hero must overcome a set of obstacles in what Northrop Frye describes as a structural movement from one form of social order to another. The path that the hero takes to reach this goal is, however, not always linear and rational, for as Calderwood and Toliver note, the comic plot "specializes in the improbable, the reversible, the redemption that comes from nowhere (deus ex machina)."[12] Further, as Levin explains, "it is the comic mandate to turn everything upside down in order that, eventually, it may be put to rights. Without these estrangements and upsets no final understanding could ever be reached."[13] The preordained happy ending presents a new, freer society, which the liberated characters celebrate with a party, wedding, or other festive ritual. The obstacles have been removed, desires have been fulfilled, and the villains, or irreconcilable characters, have been converted or summarily expelled.

Although most so-called comedies share these killjoys, obstacles, reversals, and happy endings, comedy is also and more importantly a distinct perception of human life. As Dauster explains, while tragedy "recognizes our puny human mortality," comedy recognizes "our ability to *transcend* our puniness. It is a matter of authorial point of view."[14] This capacity to transcend or to overcome corresponds to what theorist Robert Corrigan identifies as the comic view of life: "the sense that no matter how many times man is knocked down he somehow manages to pull himself up and keep on going."[15] In Carballido's case, however, the "man" is more often than not a woman. Corrigan derives this theory in part from Kierkegaard's philosophy of life as something inherently and contradictorily comic: "the comical is present in every stage of life, for wherever there is life there is contradiction, and wherever there is contradiction the comical is present."[16] Granted, Carballido has not had to look far for a steady supply of contradiction and the attendant comic element, for contradiction is an integral part of the Mexican state, from the title of the ruling party, which somehow claims to be revolutionary and institutional at the same time, to the glaring daily juxtaposition of rich and poor, educated and uneducated, urban and rural, order and chaos. These incongruities are the basis of Mexican daily reality and at the same time the mainstay of Carballido's comedies.

Given the lack of a universally recognized treatise on the nature of comedy, it is hardly surprising that theorists widely disagree as to the purpose of the genre. Some, like Sypher, see comedy as a "pleasure mechanism . . . a momentary and publicly useful resistance to authority and an escape from its pressures."[17] Others, like L. C. Knights, view comedy as a social document designed to make the audience recognize in the onstage characters its own vices and foibles.[18] Harold Watts implies a similar perception when he asserts that "comedy lets the author speak boldly in the forum. But it keeps him in the forum."[19] This last statement suggests that comedy offers a relatively safe platform from which the author can take gentle stabs at the ways and manners of a given society. It could also mean that no one in the forum takes him seriously and hence the tendency of critics to scorn comedy in favor of more "serious" forms of drama. To think of comedy solely as a source of mindless amusement is, however, a gross error, for as Benjamin Lehmann reminds us, "though we laugh at actions and utterances in comedy, we do not laugh at the comedy as a whole, for the comedy as a whole is a serious work."[20] In a similar vein, Levin notes that comedies at once register "the imprint of their times and places" and "outlive them by appealing to broad universals."[21] As will be seen, Carballido's *comedias* not only poke gentle fun at the flaws and vices of the average man and woman, but also utilize their own comicity to undermine the status quo and to raise serious questions concerning happiness, freedom, and justice.

In *Rosalba y los Llaveros*, Carballido stages a humorous cultural clash between province and capital, old and new, when cousin Rosalba blows into Otatitlán, Veracruz, with her bright, low-cut clothing, cigarettes, and frank, Freudian discourse. Accompanied by her naive and flirtatious mother, Rosalba up-ends the silent, stagnant, and sexually repressed household of Uncle Lorenzo and Aunt Lola. Almost upon arrival, she senses skeletons in the family closet and immediately sets out to find them. These family secrets revolve around her cousin, Lázaro, whom no one in the family addresses directly, a young girl named Azalea, and her mother, Luz, whom Rosalba and Aurora presume to be the maid. It does not take Rosalba long to learn that Azalea is not Lázaro's girlfriend but the product of Luz and Lázaro's childhood promiscuity. A secondary plot line involves Rosalba's other cousin, Rita, her ambiguous feelings for the socially inferior Felipe, and her extreme dislike of his vulgar sister Chole. There are also sporadic appearances of a dotty, old aunt, Nativitas, whose wanderings and ramblings, like Lázaro's unspoken sin, have caused the family no end of shame and embarrassment. A free spirit, Nativitas stands in complete contrast to her repressed relatives and thus provides the incongruity germane to the comic. This nutty aunt not only provides comic relief but also functions as a precursor of Abuela, the senile and blind "see-er" of *Fotografía en la playa,* and the town *loco* of *Un pequeño día de ira,* who is the only one crazy enough to speak the truth. No one but the audience realizes the true significance of Nativitas's declaration, "The world needs to be woken up!"[22]

By the end of act 2 and after only eight days, Rosalba has, with her pseudo-Freudian techniques, forced the family members to open their hearts as well as their mouths and thereby "solved" their problems. For instance, she has convinced Felipe that Rita suffers from an inherited form of insanity and thus persuaded him not to marry her. Lázaro, emboldened by Rosalba's encouragement to speak out, has ordered the belligerent Luz to leave the house. Rosalba is, however, eventually hoisted by her own petard, for in her effort to provide a rational, scientific explanation and solution to all their problems, she has overlooked one thing— feelings, both theirs and her own. The second act ends not with hugs and laughter but with shock, anger, and shame: Rita, furious that Rosalba has driven away her only prospect for marriage and an escape from home, reveals that Luz is expecting another child, while Rosalba tries to recover from Lázaro's shocking declaration of love and the recognition of her own reciprocal feelings.

In act 3, Carballido follows the basic conventions of comedy in allowing the complications to multiply before resolving all of them at the drop of a hat, or in this case, a few words. Before the knots of the plot can be untied, Rosalba further complicates matters by leading her aunt and uncle to the conclusion that Luz and Lázaro should be married and that Rita should go live for a while with an aunt in Veracruz. The real resolution is not, however, provided by trouble-shooter Rosalba, but by Luz herself when she declares that the second baby was not fathered, as all had blindly assumed, by Lázaro. Subsequent to this startling revelation, Luz bids them all a final "chin" as she goes off to live with her lover, Lázaro and Azalea plan to start life anew in the capital, Rosalba and Lázaro declare once again their love for one another, and Rosalba stages one last scene whereby Rita regains Felipe's devotion. The various couples unite and reunite in the prescribed happy ending, while bells, fireworks, music, and a new dawn symbolically herald the start of a new life.

Although most of the humor arises as the result of the collision of provincial manners and mores with those of the big city, the differences between the two are never resolved. As Sypher notes, "the comedian can evade the conflict, relieving the stress between competing ideals by laughter. He may enable us to 'adjust' incompatible standards without resolving the clash between them."[23] The relationships between Rosalba and Lázaro, Felipe and Rita bridge the gap between city and province, yet there is no guarantee that either of these relationships will endure. Furthermore, the dramatist presents neither province nor capital in an entirely favorable light, for like the Llaveros, Rosalba and her mother clearly have their faults. Juan Tovar notes that Rosalba, in particular, "has her own blindness, her own refuge from reality, which also gets destroyed in the course of the play. The catalyst is catalyzed."[24] If there is a winner at all, it is Lázaro, who discovers his own voice, gains freedom, and experiences love for the first time, all thanks to the efforts, however misguided and bungled, of his vivacious and liberated cousin.

The contrast between city and province is evident not only in the characters' clothing but also in their mode of discourse. Lorenzo and Lola's utterances are stiff and formal, while Rosalba is shockingly frank and her mother makes a regular habit of sticking her foot in her mouth.[25] The disparity between these forms of discourse is the source of constant humor as aunt and uncle try to stifle the liberal ideas that Aurora and Rosalba have smuggled into their household:

> *Rosalba.* Es una cierta forma de paranoia. Sin duda hay deseo de cariño insatisfecho y un complejo espectacular. Si esto es de origen sexual, como creo, se ha de haber agravado por la menopausia.
> *Lorenzo.* ¡Rita! Ve a ver a la cocina si no se quema algo.

> *Rosalba.* It is a certain type of paranoia. There is undoubtedly an unsatisfied desire for affection and a tremendous complex. If this has a sexual origin, as I believe, it must have been aggravated by menopause.
> *Lorenzo.* Rita! Go to the kitchen and see if something isn't burning.
> (*Rosalba*, 148–49)

A caricature of provincial mentality and patriarchal authority, Lorenzo concerns himself only with family honor and responsibility and with "what will the neighbors say?" Rosalba's inquiries into family affairs are continually met with nervous coughs or sudden interest in the windows and curtains:

> *Rosalba.* Quiero sentarme junto a Lázaro.
> *Lorenzo. (Tose.)* Lola, qué aire entra, cierra esa ventana.

> *Rosalba.* I want to sit next to Lázaro.
> *Lorenzo. (Coughing.)* Lola, what a breeze; close that window.
>
> (*Rosalba,* 163)

To the end, the stiff-necked Lorenzo is incapable of free speech. Rather than order Lázaro to do the right thing by marrying Luz, he utters nothing but a string of ridiculous preambles:

> Esto es, pues, Lázaro, hijo mío: debo decirte que si ves a la familia reunida es porque se reunió especialmente para un asunto de la mayor gravedad. *(Se limpia la frente. Tose un poco.)* . . . Eso es: lo que quiero decir es nada más esto: *(Se seca el sudor de las manos.)* Sale sobrando hablar de lo que ocurre, porque todos lo sabemos bien, pero . . . *(Carraspea.)* Mira, hijo, en resumen, lo poco que hay que decir es apenas lo siguiente: *(Abre la boca una o dos veces, pero calla. Al fin:)* Díselo tú, Lola.

> [Here it is, then, Lázaro, son: I must tell you that if you see the family gathered here it is because it has come together for a special matter of the greatest gravity. *(He wipes his brow and coughs a bit.)* . . . There: what I want to say is nothing more than this: *(He wipes the sweat from his hands.)* There isn't any need to talk about what is going on, because we all know it well, but . . . *(Clearing his throat.)* Look, son, in short, the little that I have to say is but the following: *(He opens his mouth one or two times, but remains silent. Finally:)* You tell him, Lola.]
>
> (*Rosalba,* 214)

Lorenzo, as Rosalba's opposite and the opposition, fits neatly into Levin's category of comic killjoy: "They cannot make a joke; they cannot take a joke; they cannot see the joke; they spoil the game. Humorless and unconsciously humorous . . . they cannot adapt their preconceptions to actuality, when it unavoidably presses upon their lives."[26]

Because of this very inability to speak, this "fear of words, of simple words" (*Rosalba,* 216), and their resistance to change, Lola and Lorenzo end up being the only real losers and appear merely as marginal members of the final society. In typical comedic structure, the original society, "controlled by habit, ritual bondage, arbitrary law and the older characters," gives way, according to Northrop Frye, to "a society controlled by youth and pragmatic freedom." As the epitome of the original society, Lorenzo fits Frye's descriptions of humor as "someone with a lot of social prestige and power, who is able to force much of the play's society into line with his obsession."[27] Lola, as the traditional sidekick, echoes her husband's words and even follows his hilarious habit of avoiding painful issues by busying herself with windows and curtains. While seemingly trivial matters, the windows and their covers serve as effective visual signs of provincial hermeticism, the characters' inability to speak freely, and their desire to keep these dirty little secrets within the four walls of the family home.

Rosalba, like her uncle, is incapable of change. Instead of learning a lesson from all the chaos she has unleashed within the family, she continues to the end to manipulate those around her. Before the curtain closes, she stages mock heartbreak at the piano to lure Lázaro back to her and concocts an absurd story of attempted suicide to reunite Felipe with Rita. She remains the consummate actress, acutely aware of playing a role despite the disastrous effects she has produced. Yet neither her histrionic talents nor her university education ultimately provides the solution to the family problems. While she does manage to bring these problems out into the light—"I love the light" (*Rosalba*, 191)—she merely exacerbates them by stimulating and manipulating the characters' emotions without giving any thought to the consequences. She is a feminine and ironic version of what Calderwood and Toliver term the "interior dramatist," who stations the players, orders the plot, and creates with his magical "art" the comic spectacle. "Through him we become conscious of . . . the controlling dramatist 'outside' the play, who, in fidelity to the comic form, is maneuvering everything towards desired ends."[28] Through her manipulation of Lázaro, in particular, Rosalba effects a reversal of the Hollywood master plan: girl meets boy, girl loses boy, and girl gets boy. Moreover, in Carballido's ironic version of the comic heroine, the characters' problems are resolved not because of Rosalba, but in *spite* of her. For all her claims to culture and knowledge—"there is a solution for everything" (*Rosalba*, 161)—she winds up looking thoroughly ridiculous.

The issues that Rosalba pushes onto center stage—sexual freedom and repression, social and racial prejudices—were still quite taboo in 1950. Carballido's incorporation of these social and moral concerns into the comedic structure reflects more than a glimmer of Rodolfo Usigli, who, in turn, was heavily influenced by George Bernard Shaw and his combination of comedy and social criticism.[29] More than real beings of flesh and blood, the figures that inhabit *Rosalba* are representative of particular values and social groups. As Dauster notes, these characters are "consciously created to exemplify something."[30] The names Rosalba and Aurora, for example, convey their illuminating function within the obscurity of the household and its hidden relationships. Both women represent language and action amidst the darkness and silence that govern the household. Although Rita and Felipe may initially seem extraneous to the main plot, they are key to this dramatic "upgrading" as the primary vehicle through which Carballido portrays the racial and social barriers that often impede human communication. Rita clearly loves Felipe, but she has been raised to see those of his class as "ugly, Indian, vulgar, sloppy" (*Rosalba*, 162). From the top of the social scale, she shares her parents' belief that social class is more important than moral class, while Luz and Chole, with their course features and speech, occupy the lower rung. In social limbo, we find Felipe, who has gained an education at the expense of Chole's youth and dignity, Azalea, who is at once the granddaughter of Lola and Lorenzo and the daughter of the maid, and Lázaro, to whom no family member has spoken since Luz's latest pregnancy was detected.

Although the characters lean toward caricature and/or social types, *Rosalba* is technically a realistic comedy. Carballido shows an early fine eye for realistic detail in the setting, costumes, physical appearance of the characters, and their gestures and movements. The proliferation of short scenes in each act—thirty-six in act 2 alone—underscores the upheaval that Rosalba has provoked in the household, as the characters continually enter and exit the stage in a constant effort to avoid one another. Among the many visual signs contained in an elaborately realistic setting, the most noteworthy are the scores of family portraits and the number of mirrors that dot the walls. While the smiling, youthful faces contained in the portraits suggest familial well-being and unity, the mirrors reflect their true faces of distrust, disappointment, and resentment. The latter are the countenances that the characters must confront when the truth is finally spoken. All action, or rather inaction, is contained within the living room, which is normally a scene of socialization. In this case, however, it is the scenario for strained dialogue at best and a place where the characters symbolically "hide" forbidden topics of conversation behind the closed and oft-mentioned windows and curtains.

Although *Rosalba* may seem a bit quaint for a modern audience accustomed to onstage violence, sex, and sensationalism, it nonetheless offers a compassionate and nostalgic view of midcentury Mexico. Carballido establishes here the structural pattern, the character types, the mixture of humor and social concerns, and the tonal joie de vivre for the comedies to follow. Rosalba, Lorenzo, Lázaro, and Nativitas, for example, will reappear in different settings, dramatic genres, and guises throughout his long comedic career. *Rosalba* deserves to be remembered not only as Carballido's first successful experiment with comedy but also as Mexico's first modern comedy in its perfect blend of provincial manners, technical realism, gentle humor, and irony. Like all the other dramatic genres with which he has experimented, Carballido established in *Rosalba* his own unique brand of comedy.

During the four decades that followed the writing and staging of *Rosalba*, Carballido tried on a variety of dramatic styles and genres, many of which he blended together in works of increasingly greater originality and complexity. By the time he returned to comedy in *Rosa de dos aromas*, the years of experimentation had led him to abandon realism for a denser and more expressionistic style of representation. Furthermore, the years of writing short prose fiction had taught him to economize in words, actions, and characters.[31] As a result, *Rosa* provides the same compassionate and gentle humor of the earlier comedies but with the concision, deftness, and originality of a seasoned dramatist.

In *Rosa de dos aromas*, Carballido employs a highly condensed structure and dialogue to revisit many of the same questions he planted in *Rosalba*. The large casts of his early comedies have been pared down to just two characters—two women—while the representatives of patriarchal authority—their shared husband/lover, lawyer, and combined five sons—exist but offstage. It is highly significant that the husband/lover and cause of the comic complication now remains on the margin, out of view, while his former, passive objects evolve into subjects and directors of their own fate.[32] Like Mina and Fifí of Carballido's *Orinoco*, Marlene and Gabriela are conscious of this promotion to directors and at the same time perfect incarnations of Carballido's ideal actress: "I like women who have the ovaries to act, who eat up the spotlight, who tear down the curtains, and who know how to shout."[33]

The three long acts and detailed realism of his earlier comedies give way here to one long act in nine scenes. This single act is framed by two surprising revelations. The first occurs in a prison waiting room, where Gabriela and Marlene initiate a conversation while awaiting a visit with their husband and "man," respectively. A simple dialogue based on marital status, children, and family life leads to the inevitable discovery that they have come to visit the same man, who has not only led a secret, double life but also has been imprisoned for having sexual relations with yet another woman, in this case a minor. In this modern inversion of the traditional triangle, two women make claims for the same man. Yet, despite their initial contempt for one another, Gabriela and Marlene gradually recognize that they must work together if they are to perform their conjugal duty and produce the one million pesos they need to "buy" his release from prison. Enmity gives way to camaraderie as they join forces in organizing huge lotteries and raffles. Yet as the money begins to accumulate, the women grow increasingly cynical of their "duty" and even begin indulging themselves with a few luxuries. When an accident produces a monetary setback, "las señoras de Lesur" again resort to their own wit and manipulate Tony/Maco into using his entire pension to pay for a good part of his own release. In a shared comic anagnorisis, Marlene and Gabriela arrive simultaneously at the recognition that they owe Tony/Maco absolutely nothing and that, on the contrary, he owes them. As the curtain falls, the two women dance, laugh, and plan a lengthy and extravagant beach vacation, leaving their former beloved to rot in prison. The final celebratory scene of song, dance, and drunken laughter follows the same pattern of sacrifice and feast that was used in ancient ritual and the earliest of comedies. As self-appointed goddesses, Marlene and Gabriela "sacrifice" Tony/Maco and feast on the offering that he has unwittingly made to them.

The delightful humor of *Rosa de dos aromas* derives not only from the unexpected twists that occur in the opening and final scenes, but also from the incongruous, forced union of Gabriela and Marlene. As Sypher explains, "comedy is built upon double occasions, double premises, double values," and the humor arises from the distance between the doubled elements.[34] In this distilled comedy, there are two very different women, two Marco Antonio Lesurs (Maco and Tony), and two standards of conduct—one male and one female—which provide the requisite incongruities. As Marlene and Gabriela unwittingly await a visit with the same man, visual and verbal signs suggest that they share neither social class nor lifestyle. Gabriela reads and takes notes from a large technical book, while Marlene mistakes the book for a novel and fusses over her nails and hair. Gabriela, the wife, is a professional translator and high school teacher while Marlene, a beauty salon operator, has produced two illegitimate children with two different fathers. Gabriela is university educated, cultured, and well read—from Freud to José Agustín—while Marlene is still unsure how to pronounce her own name. Despite these blatant social differences, however, the two women come to realize that they share not only Marco Antonio Lesur but also their status as women/objects in a male-dominated society.

As Marlene and Gabriela uncover their common bond, they undergo a transformation from object to subject and from actress to director. This metamorphosis is most evident in the changing pattern of their discourse. The dialogue slowly evolves from barely contained rage and dismissal to a forced and formal cordiality, and finally to the *tuteo* of two old pals. Halfway through the play, in a pivotal fifth scene, the two women become virtually indistinguishable when their simultaneous phone "monologues" show both of them using the same wit, flattery, and deceit to sell raffle tickets to their friends and clients. As Marlene and Gabriela drop the social masks that society has issued them, they discover the joys of free discourse. Following a feast of pork loin, wine, and a liberal dose of rum, the newfound pals unleash years of repressed anger and resentment in a cathartic session of creative name-calling:

Marlene. Para qué nombraste al hijo de la chingada. Estábamos tan contentas . . .
(Pausita.)
Gabriela. Hijo de puta, sub-ojete.
(Pausita.)
Marlene. Pendejo de mierda.

. . . .

Gabriela. Infraenano, traidor, pseudomarxista, pedorro. *(Pausita.)* Orale, tú sigues.
Marlene. No, mana, me la pusiste difícil. Besaculos de ricos, priísta, lambiscón, pocoshuevos. Vas tú.

. . . .

(Carcajadas de ambas.)

[*Marlene.* Why'd you have to bring up that sonofabitch! We were having so much fun. . . .
(Brief pause.)
Gabriela. Bastard. Asshole.

(Brief pause.)
Marlene. Shit.

. . . . .

Gabriela. Neanderthal, swindler, pseudo-Marxist, fartface.
(Brief pause.) Come on, your turn.
Marlene. Oh . . . Gabi, you're making it too hard. Ass-kisser, right-winger, brown nose, pencil-penis. Now you.

. . . .

(Howls of laughter from both.)][35]

As Marlene and Gabriela liberate themselves from conventional expectations and imposed notions of female obligation, their discourse becomes progressively more open, daring, and in that sense, incongruous with the expected speech of a "lady." On a separate occasion, Carballido has stated that a true woman is "one who knows how to use the whole vocabulary . . . The poor, middle-class women are the ones who have not only their lives, but also their vocabulary half-mutilated."[36] On a similar note, Octavio Paz describes these "bad words" as "the only live language in a world of anemic words.[37] There is an infectious delight here as the obscenities become progressively coarser and the ladylike giggles evolve into roars of drunken laughter. Prior to the publication and performance of *Rosa de dos aromas*, Cypess noted the same kind of liberation-through-discourse in *Rosalba y los Llaveros* and *El día que se soltaron los leones*. With regard to the latter, she explains that "Ana had previously been the victim of a manipulative, authoritarian moral code and its concomitant restrictive discursive practices. Her present discursive transgressions now reveal her disdain for that society and her liberation from it."[38] By entering the forbidden territory of male-only discourse, Marlene and Gabriela score a victory, albeit verbal, over years of patriarchal domination. They carry the liberation one step further than Ana did, for while *Leones* ends with Ana in the lions' cage, it is Maco/Tony who remains behind bars as the curtain falls on *Rosa de dos aromas*.

Although this piece is predominantly light in tone, there are moments when Marlene and Gabriela look past their immediate circumstances to their situation as women in a male-oriented and dominated society. They gradually reach the conclusion that true love is difficult, if not impossible, given that the effort and commitment of one partner are rarely matched by the other. Their self-conscious discoveries range from the humorous to the deeply cynical. In a monologue of drunken self-pity, for example, Gabriela decides that the only respectable and rewarding relationship that a woman can have with a man would be as the widow of a dead one:

> No es bonito tener la casa llena de hijos de presidiario. Huérfanos, sí sería bonito. Es elegante ser viuda. Qué ilusión, toda de negro, muy respetable . . . Porque vivir soltera, es una vergüenza; casada . . . ya sabemos. Divorciada . . . eso no dura; y puros corajes, pleitos legales; como despegar resistol. Arrejuntada: eso está bien para viejas patanas, como la peluquera. Lo único limpio y bello es la viudez.

> [A house filled with the kids of a jailbird isn't much fun. Now, orphans, that would be fine. It's elegant to be a widow. A vision in black, totally respectable. Widowhood, it's wonderful! Somehow it's shameful to be an old maid; and a married woman . . . we know how that is. Divorced . . . that doesn't last long, and it's nothing but anger and legal tangles, worse than getting unstuck from Crazy Glue. Mistress? That's for peasants like the beautician broad. The only good, clean way to go is to be widowed.]

> (*Rosa*, 77/13)

Later, she cynically concludes that the absolute best one can do with a live spouse is "saberse de antemano el repertorio de por-querías que te pueden hacer" [knowing in advance the whole shitty bag of tricks they can play on you"] (*Rosa*, 97/22). As a result of their intimate dialogues, Marlene and Gabriela come to recognize Tony/Maco as a mere representative of an entire social order that has to this point determined the course of their lives. Even from behind prison walls he continues to dominate their lives until they finally shake the shackles of traditional standards and patterns of behavior. The vengeance that they wreak on him is really directed toward an entire society of men that will not let them be.

It is no surprise that women often take the lead role in comedy, for, as Lehmann observes, "from Aristophanes on, comedy stands for freedom, freedom to *be*."[39] Over the years and throughout his comedies, Carballido has shown a concern with this "freedom to be," particularly with regard to women. Since comedy tradition-ally entails a move from some form of ritual or traditional bond-age to liberty, it seems a logical genre for the liberation, albeit fictitious, of the female. As Maurice Charney explains, "we all know the social rules that relegate women to a passive role, yet comedy . . . is in many ways a celebration of the power and the wit of women."[40]

Throughout Carballido's dramatic career, we find women of all ages making the break, or at least *trying* to make the break, with long-established values and norms. Gabriela and Marlene are but a more modern, more victorious, and more self-aware version of Rosalba, Rocío and Aminta, and Ana. In a short endnote to the text, fellow dramatist Luisa Josefina Hernández celebrates Marlene and Gabriela's final act as "a course of action . . . that many women have already imagined but which not all would dare to choose" (*Rosa*, 111) and implies that the play functions as a form of wish fulfillment for its female audience. In *Rosalba y los Llaveros,* the female protagonist attempts to liberate both men and women from a tradition-bound society through what Solomon Tilles calls "la palabra." Unfortunately, Rosalba does not invent a new discourse but resorts to the thoroughly patriarchal discourse of Freud to "free" her repressed relatives and consequently fails to free anyone but Lázaro. In *La danza que sueña la tortuga,* Rocío and Aminta are too old and too inculcated with traditional values to free themselves significantly in any way from Víctor's paternalistic clutches. As Víctor's successor, Tony/Maco has likewise kept two women at the same time and produced offspring with each. Unlike the modern Gabriela, however, Víctor's wife knew about his "refacción" but was such a "santa" that she never mentioned it. In *Leones,* yet another rebellious spinster, Ana, rebels against patriarchal order. The "liberation" that she ultimately attains, however, is limited by the bars of the lions' cages and ambiguous at best.

Unlike most of their comic predecessors, Marlene and Gabriela live in the capital and work as professionals. They are both, in a sense, modern single moms, who somehow manage to hold down a job and raise their children. They have rum to help them through the difficult moments and tranquilizers for when the going really gets rough. Yet, while they enjoy a certain amount of comfort and financial independence, the sad fact is that neither can live without men. Although Marlene and Gabriela are clearly more triumphant than their female antecedents, their determination to head to the beach "que esté más llena . . . ¡De galanes, de galanes, de galanes!" [that's fullest . . . BOTH of studs! Studs! STUDS! (*Rosa*, 110/29) is a sobering and conciliatory reminder that life with men is better than no life at all.

Stripped of all the realistic and costumbristic trappings and the extraneous characters of the early comedies, *Rosa de dos aromas* represents the simplest and purest of Carballido's comedies. In its comic condensation, it follows the evolution of modern comedy, which has, as Arthur Koestler explains, "increasingly to rely for

its effects on a change from caricature to witticism, from the
comic of situations to brilliant dialogue."[41] Witty and bold dialogue is indeed the key to the success of Carballido's longest-
running play. Whereas sex was certainly a taboo topic in the Llavero household, and, to a certain extent, on the whole Mexican
stage of the 1950s, it is the main topic of discussion in *Rosa de dos
aromas*. Here, however, the emphasis is on sex as gender rather
than on sex as act. In this thoroughly modern version of *La danza*'s
Aminta and Rocío, Carballido packs the house with his compassionate and comic portrayal of certain gender-related types with
which the contemporary audience is all too familiar—the adulter-
ous *macho*, the single mom, the professional woman, and the corrupt lawyer. More than just a simple case of male-bashing,
Carballido holds up for the male as well as the female audience
a comically distorted reflection of the absurd norms and double
standards that dictate the sexual conduct of women as well as men
in contemporary Mexican society.[42]

In an essay entitled "Whatever Happened to Comedy?" Richard
Duprey laments the virtual disappearance of comedy on today's
stage. The reason, he maintains, is that "if there are no generally
held social norms, then there can be no great comedy. The break
from the norm has no meaning unless there is a commonly held
norm from which to break."[43] Levin suggests the same phenomenon but attributes it to "the importance of becoming serious, the
decline of occasions to celebrate, the dismissal of fun as unwar-
ranted frivolity."[44] Carballido's frequent recourse to comedy and
his lasting concern with female emancipation prove, however, that
the serious and the comic blend well and that there is still at
least one norm generally held among Mexicans and that is the
traditional acceptance of male domination and the attendant double standard. Furthermore, in regretting the loss of widely held
norms and the concomitant death of comedy, Duprey overlooks
the other major ingredient in the genre, which is incongruity. It
seems safe to say that as long as the oppositions of female/male,
rural/urban, educated/ignorant, corrupt/naive, wealthy/poor remain in the foreground of Mexican society, there will be plenty
of fodder for comic theatre. Over the years, Carballido returns to
this pervasive and persistent social reality, treating it with humor,
compassion, and insight. While *Rosalba* and *Rosa* vary tremen-
dously in structure, plot, and technique, both significantly end
with liberation, celebration, and hope for the future. More than
just stock types, his characters are human, lovable creatures with
whom we sympathize, if not empathize, in their struggle to be

happy, free, and loved. Although many of their preoccupations are universal concerns, these characters are profoundly Mexican in their customs, values, and language. Carballido's comedies, like other "great comedies," demonstrate and celebrate humankind's ability to endure and to overcome the daily, inescapable difficulty of being. Corrigan believes that "in a time when our next tomorrow must always be in question, comedy's tenacious greed for life, its instinct for self-preservation, and its attempts to mediate the pressures of our daily life seem to qualify it as the most appropriate mode for the drama of the mid-twentieth century."[45] In both *Rosalba* and *Rosa*, Carballido at once leads his audience to laughter and forces them to acknowledge the serious, inescapable oppositions that form the basis of daily Mexican reality. At the same time, he proves that comedy is far from dead.

Notes

1. Carballido actually wrote six others plays before *Rosalba y los Llaveros*, five of which are one-acts. The one full-length play, *Los dos mundos de Alberta*, was sentenced by Carballido himself to oblivion.

2. Frank Dauster, *Historia del teatro hispanoamericano* (Mexico: Ediciones de Andrea, 1966), 101; translation mine.

3. *Rosalba* and *Rosa* represent, respectively, the first and latest of Carballido's comedies. In between these two works, he wrote a number of other comedies, including *La danza que sueña la tortuga* (1954), *Un vals sin fin sobre el planeta* (begun in 1957; completed and staged in 1970), and most of the one-act pieces that comprise the various collections entitled *D.F.*

4. *Rosalba y los Llaveros* was recently re-staged in Mexico City (12–16 July 1994) at the Universidad Pedagógica Nacional under the direction of Carballido and Froylán Cuenca.

5. With the notable exception of *Comedy: Meaning and Form*, ed. Robert Corrigan (San Francisco: Chandler, 1965), there are few lengthy treatises on traditional comedy. On the other hand, the past two decades have seen a proliferation of studies on what has alternately been called "modern comedy," "dark comedy," "tragicomedy," and "tragifarce." See, in particular: J. L. Styan, *Dark Comedy: The Development of Modern Comic Tragedy* (London: Cambridge University Press, 1968); Robert Corrigan, *The Theatre in Search of a Fix* (New York: Delta, 1973); Maurice Charney, *Comedy High and Low: An Introduction to the Experience of Comedy* (New York: Oxford University Press, 1978); and Harry Levin, ed., *Veins of Humor* (Cambridge: Harvard University Press, 1972).

6. Frank Dauster, *Ensayos sobre teatro hispanoamericano* (Mexico: Sep-Setentas, 1975), 147; translation mine.

7. Suzanne Langer, "The Comic Rhythm," in *Comedy*, 131.

8. James Calderwood and Harold Toliver, *Perspectives on Drama* (London: Oxford University Press, 1968), 163.

9. Willie Sypher, "The Meanings of Comedy," in *Comedy*, 30.

10. Harry Levin, *Playboys and Killjoys: An Essay on the Theory and Practice of Comedy* (New York: Oxford University Press, 1987), 36.

11. Sypher, "Meanings of Comedy," 49.

12. Calderwood and Toliver, *Perspectives*, 164.

13. Levin, *Playboys*, 102.
14. Frank Dauster, "Toward a Definition of Tragedy," *Revista Canadiense de Estudios Hispánicos* 7 (Fall 1982): 11.
15. Corrigan, *Comedy*, 3.
16. Ibid., 20.
17. Sypher, "Meanings of Comedy," 50.
18. L. C. Knights, "Notes on Comedy," in *Comedy*, 186.
19. Harold Watts, "The Sense of Regain: A Theory of Comedy," in *Comedy*, 192.
20. Benjamin Lehmann, "Comedy and Laughter," in *Comedy*, 164.
21. Levin, *Playboys*, 5.
22. Emilio Carballido, *Rosalba y los Llaveros*, in *Teatro* (Mexico: Fondo de Cultura Económica, 1965), 206. Hereafter *Rosalba*, cited in the text, with reference numbers referring to *Teatro*.
23. Sypher, "Meanings of Comedy," 52.
24. Juan Tovar, "Presentación: Homenaje a Emilio Carballido," *Letras de Veracruz* 1 (1973): 5; translation mine.
25. In his study on the use of language in *Rosalba*, Solomon H. Tilles describes in more detail the family's inability and/or fear to engage in dialogue: "Por estar tan conscientes y tener tanto miedo al diálogo, no se afirman en casi nada; al contrario, se niegan la palabra"; in "La importancia de 'la palabra' en *Rosalba y los Llaveros*," *Latin American Theatre Review* 8 (Spring 1975):41. Furthermore, he notes Rosalba's use of "la palabra" as a weapon in asserting her control over the lives of her reticent relatives. The flaw in his argument is that he reduces the dramatic conflict to a question of existential psychology, thus negating the social and cultural implications of the misunderstandings and complications among the characters. In a later study, Sandra Messinger Cypess takes another look at the issue of discourse and applies Foucault's three principles of exclusion, limitation, and appropriation to the dialogues and power struggles that occur among the characters in *Rosalba*. She notes, in particular, that in her discourse Rosalba personifies "the masculine characteristics of authority, reason, and analysis"; in "i, Too, Speak: 'Female' Discourse in Carballido's Plays," *Latin American Theatre Review* 18 (Fall 1984):48. It is, indeed, Rosalba's unsuccessful appropriation of patriarchal discursive practices that leads to her failure to solve the characters' problems.
26. Levin, *Playboys*, 38.
27. Northrop Frye, "The Mythos of Spring; Comedy," in *Comedy*, 147.
28. Calderwood and Toliver, *Perspectives*, 175.
29. *Rosalba* reveals not only the influence of Carballido's mentor, Rodolfo Usigli, in its attention to realistic detail, but also that of his contemporaries, particularly Celestino Gorostiza and Luisa Josefina Hernández, whose *El color de nuestra piel* and *Los frutos caídos* share a similar concern with social mores in their realistic treatment of racial prejudice and the intrusion of urban values into the provincial way of life.
30. Frank Dauster, "*Fotografía en la playa: Rosalba* a los treinta años," paper presented at Rollins College, February 1985, 3; translation mine.
31. Although Carballido is widely known as a dramatist, his prose fiction has received very little attention. To date, his prose production includes several novellas and a collection of short stories entitled *La caja vacía*. Several of these stories have served as the basis for full-length dramas, such as *¡Silencio, pollos pelones, ya les van a echar su maíz!* and *Un vals sin fin sobre el planeta*. In general, Carballido's narrative works display the same concision and emphasis on atmosphere and dialogue that are found in his theatre.
32. Frank Dauster observes that *Rosa* is strikingly similar to *Orinoco*, which preceded it by only four years: "owing in great measure to their friendship, two female victims of a limited, critical, *machista* situation find sufficient inner strength to declare their indepen-

144 PERSPECTIVES ON CONTEMPORARY SPANISH AMERICAN THEATRE

dence"; in "Carballido y el teatro de la liberación," *Alba de América* 7 (July 1989):218–19; translation mine. There are also more specific parallels, as he notes: a nonrealistic setting; the low verbal humor that accompanies their relative liberation; and the juxtaposition of opposite modes of perception (219). This same opposition, however, constitutes the dramatic conflict and primary source of humor in *Orinoco*, as the women combat against an almost certain destiny, whereas in *Rosa* individual differences in lifestyle are soon put behind in Marlene and Gabriela's common struggle against the "enemy."

33. Tomás Espinosa, "Emilio Carballido: Una entrevista," in *Orinoco. Las cartas de Mozart. Felicidad* (Mexico: Editores Mexicanos Unidos, 1985), 256; translation mine.

34. Sypher, "Meanings of Comedy," 32.

35. Emilio Carballido, *Rosa de dos aromas* (Mexico: Editores Mexicanos Unidos, 1986), 94–95. The English translation is by Margaret Sayers Peden, *A Rose, By Any Other Names* . . ., in *Modern International Drama* 22 (Fall 1988):20–21. Hereafter *Rosa*, cited in the text. All quotations in Spanish are from the Unidos edition of *Rosa*, and all translations are from Peden's *A Rose;* page numbers carried are for both the Spanish and English versions of the play.

36. In Espinosa, "Emilio Carballido," 247.

37. Octavio Paz, *Laberinto de la soledad* (Mexico: Fondo de Cultura Económica, 1959), 67; translation mine.

38. Cypess, "I, Too, Speak," 50.

39. Lehmann, "Comedy and Laughter," 167.

40. Charney, *Comedy High and Low*, 90.

41. Arthur Koestler, "Comedy," in *Comedy*, 215.

42. Conversely, Carballido has been accused of advancing *machista* attitudes in *Rosa*, to which he responds in an interview with Rubén Ríos Avila: "No way is this a *machista* play. It deals simply with two women with riotous behavior, who are unrespectable and in no way worthy of imitation. It is obvious that the play does not correspond to what the women say; it is a comic work and the final scene, when they finally change their minds, has proven to be very cathartic for the Mexican women who have seen it"; in "Conversando con Carballido," *El Mundo* [San Juan], 28 August 1988, 15.

43. Richard Duprey, "Whatever Happened to Comedy?" in *Comedy*, 245.

44. Levin, *Playboys*, 115.

45. Corrigan, *Comedy*, 2.

Tragedy and Marginality in José Triana's *Medea en el espejo*

William García
Union College

THE texts of the Greek tragedians, Aeschylus, Sophocles, and Euripides, constitute an ever-influential body of dramatic literature, with a great impact and attraction within the hegemonic canon of Western literature. Many of the tragedies created by the classical Greek playwrights have been adapted and recreated by writers throughout the centuries, such as Seneca, Racine, Hofmannsthal, Cocteau, Giraudoux, Sartre, Anouilh, and O'Neill, among the most famous. An unknown fact to many authors of world drama histories is that the Latin American playwrights have not been oblivious to the rewriting of tragic myths originally elaborated by the Greeks. In an article on Greek myth and contemporary Latin American theatre, Costa Palamides points out that among the numerous and diverse themes, trends, and subjects within the vast, but quite unknown, Latin American dramaturgy, the classical Greek myth is one of the most employed.[1] The extended list of Latin American plays based on Greek tragedies enables us to speak of a practice. This array of theatrical pieces, ranging from *Ifigenia cruel* (Mexico, 1923) by Alfonso Reyes to *Antígona furiosa* (Argentina, 1986) by Griselda Gambaro, supports the vogue of the Greek myth as a constant theme in the Latin American theatre.[2] The critical attention paid to this practice has definitely been limited, which should not be surprising given the undeserved lack of international recognition and common critical devalorization of the Latin American theatre.

The marginalization of Latin American plays by the hegemonic canon, with its centers in Europe and the United States, poses as obvious the inclusion of Anouilh's *Médée* and Robinson Jeffers's *Medea* in world drama histories, and the exclusion of, for example, *Medea en el espejo* (Medea in the mirror) by Cuban playwright José

Triana. Actually, in the annals of world drama, none of the Latin American versions of the myth of Medea are mentioned: *La selva* (Peru, 1950) by Juan Ríos, *Malintzin (Medea americana)* (Mexico, 1957) by Jesús Sotelo Inclán, *Gota d'Agua* (Brazil, 1982) by Chico Buarque and Paulo Pontes, *Ma'Déa* (1985) by French-Cuban dramatist Eduardo Manet, and *Medea de Moquehua* (Argentina, 1992) by Luis María Salvaneschi. Latin American playwrights who rewrite classical tragedies have to deal with the canonical conventions of the genre, establishing—consciously or not, regardless of their political or theatrical discourse—a textual dialogue with a theatrical canon that persists in disregarding their work. The present study of José Triana's version of Euripides' *Medea* focuses on the theme of marginality, which the dramatist examines not only in terms of race and social status but also at a cultural level, since the situation of his heroine parallels that of the text, a "barbarian" text struggling at the margin of the polis of the canon. In *Medea en el espejo* Triana shares three key concerns with other Latin American playwrights who recreate the story of Medea: the Americanization of the myth; the apparent impulse to dissociate from previous European adaptations through a different theatrical conception and a more overtly political discourse; and the attempt to reconcile a revisionist approach to the myth with the tragic dimension presented by Euripides. Triana achieves in his play a balance between a tragic formulation of the myth, an innovative and experimental theatrical proposal, and the creation of an original text deeply rooted in the social and cultural realities of the Caribbean.

José Triana, born in Cuba in 1931, started staging his plays at the beginning of the sixties, in the midst of the cultural enthusiasm of the early period of the Cuban Revolution,[3] after years of exile during the last part of the Batista regime. Frank Dauster appraises Triana's dramatic work "as essentially tragic, if tragedy is the presentation of a human being at a crucial moment of his existence, at the moment of critical choice."[4] *Medea en el espejo* and *El mayor general hablará de teogonía* (The major general will speak of theogony) were produced in 1960. Triana experimented again with the classical model of the tragedy in *La muerte del Ñeque* (The death of the Ñeque, 1963), a ritualistic piece containing the ludic symbolism of later plays.[5] In 1965, Triana won the prestigious Casa de las Américas Award with *La noche de los asesinos* (Night of the assassins), premiered the following year at the VII Festival of Latin American Theatre. Characterized by its innovation of dramatic form, this play is, among its various readings, a reflection on the nature of revolution and a rejection of authority.[6] The play, which brought international critical recognition to Triana, also marked the beginning of a period of silence that ended with his definitive exile in France in 1980. Among Triana's plays premiered or published after leaving Cuba are *Palabras comunes* (Words apart, 1986) and *Ceremonial de guerra* (War Ceremony, 1990), the latter being a rewriting of Aeschylus' *The Seven against Thebes*. Triana's adoption of European dramatic models and formulas must be examined closely. Diana Taylor argues that Triana "converts First World artistic products into vehicles for the expression of his own specific cultural and historical concerns."[7] His theatre is also characterized by its tendency to portray characters of the lower socioeconomic classes, besieged by a hostile, irrational, and violent environment.[8]

Triana's *Medea en el espejo* is representative of Latin American plays based on Greek tragedies, since it introduces a series of differentiating elements that establish a rupture with the classical text and, subsequently, keep the Latin American play at a distance from the hegemonic canon. The play develops the conflict of María, a mulatto woman abandoned by her white-skinned lover (Julián), who decides to marry the daughter of the corrupt local political boss, Perico Piedra Fina. To guarantee having Julián as an ally in his political intrigues, Perico proposes to him the marriage to his daughter Esperancita, and Julián accepts knowing he will take advantage of his new social status. María poisons Perico and his daughter during the wedding festivities and then kills her children to punish Julián and to cut all bonds with him. The parallels with Euripides' *Medea*, such as the general outline of the plot, the role of some characters within the dramatic action, and the intervention of a chorus, are attenuated by crucial differentiating elements: the protagonist's struggle to define her Afro-Caribbean identity; the presence of Afro-Cuban music and religion; the leitmotivs of gossip and Cuban *bachata* (an irreverent and mocking attitude or behavior); and the self-reference in the text. In addition, the intertextuality with Euripides' *Medea*, a canonical text, is marked by parody and a metacritical discourse.

The theme of marginality plays a noteworthy role in Latin American versions of the myth of Medea, but it is of paramount importance in *Medea en el espejo*. It introduces an ideological discourse that situates the dramatic action in the historical and cultural context of the Caribbean. By locating the action in Latin America, Triana as well as other Latin American dramatists who recreate the story of Medea, all go beyond, purposely or not, the

Americanization of the myth—in some cases, the objective of the change of location—and formulate the tragic conflict of the heroine from a new perspective. In the classical tragedy, Medea is a foreigner, betrayed and abandoned in the Greek polis (Corinth). Euripides did not overlook the marginal state of his protagonist and, through the character of the Nurse, stresses this dimension of Medea's situation:

> In silent anguish, with her snowy neck
> Averted, for her sire, her native land,
> And home, which she forsaking hither came
> With him who scorns her now. She from her woes
> Too late hath learnt how enviable the lot
> Of those who leave not their paternal roof.[9]

Medea's otherness, as a woman and as an outsider of unacceptable customs for the Greeks, did not go unnoticed for the poetic genius of Euripides. In later versions of the myth, the character of Medea is not treated sympathetically, resulting at times in the simplistic portrayal of the barbarian witch, a despicable killer crazed by jealousy. In Latin American adaptations, Medea is not a foreigner; instead she is depicted as a person marginalized within her own culture, in her native land. The sense of grievance by the Latin American Medeas is linked to the perception of their marginality.

Even if the motivation behind most of the Latin American versions of classical tragedies is the attempt to Americanize and to bring the myth up to date,[10] an analysis of the differences between the Greek tragedy and the Latin American play might be necessary to disclose the theatrical and sociopolitical discourses supporting the new version of the myth. Such differences ought to be analyzed within the cultural context in which the text is produced, reflecting on the particular modes of theatrical production and grasping the specificity of the Latin American theatrical discourse.[11] The sociopolitical and the cultural references in Triana's *Medea en el espejo* have not been ignored by the critics: Ramón V. de la Campa pinpoints the frame of the dramatic action in the prerevolutionary Cuban society; Frank Dauster discusses the influences from and its connection with other Cuban plays, Virgilio Piñera's *Electra Garrigó* (1948), Carlos Felipe's *Requiem por Yarini* (1960), and José R. Brene's *El gallo de San Isidro* (1964); and, José A. Escarpanter links Triana's play to the tradition of *bufo* theater (farce), specifically to its popular variant, the Cuban operetta *(zar-*

zuela), in which the plot of a mulatto woman abandoned by a white lover was not uncommon.[12] The particularities of *Medea en el espejo*—the elements differentiating the play from Euripides' tragedy—not only denote its sociopolitical and cultural context, but also disclose a critical response to the hegemonic canon.[13]

In *Medea en el espejo*, María's sense of identity has been distorted by the oppressive and racist ideology legitimized in her society; ironically, the lack of a truthful racial and social identity is what leads the protagonist to the extreme circumstances, thus forcing her to acknowledge her marginal state and to assert her Afro-Caribbean identity, the first steps toward casting off the shackles of oppression and racism.[14] María's tragic conflict is rooted in her incapability to accept her own identity as a Cuban mulatto woman and to value herself as a human being, defining her existence on the basis of her relationship with her blond lover, Julián:

> Me paso la vida repitiendo tu nombre. . . . Julián me ama. Julián es mi marido. Julián es el padre de mis hijos. Mi destino es Julián. . . . ¿Qué me importa lo que soy y lo que era, qué me importa la libertad, si soy la dueña de tus brazos?. . . Estos días de separación me han servido de mucho. He comprendido que eres y sólo tú la razón de mi vida. Trataré de ser más complaciente.

> [I go through life repeating your name. . . . Julián loves me. Julián is my husband. Julián is the father of my children. My destiny is Julián. . . . What do I care who I am and who I was, what do I care about freedom if I am the master of your embrace?. . . This separation has been worth it. I have realized that you, and only you, are the reason of my existence. I'll try to be more indulgent.][15]

María refuses to admit the fact that Julián has used her, mistreated her, scorned her, and left her to marry Esperancita, who, besides being the daughter of the unscrupulous political boss, is a white woman. The protagonist also rejects the thought of Julián being responsible, as Perico is, for the deaths of her father and her brother, which she has sworn to avenge (*Medea*, 30). María does not want to grasp her marginality, much less to reaffirm her identity, since it would require of her to be an active player of her existence and to make a stand against Julián, who represents, along with Perico Piedra Fina, corrupted and racist social values. The chorus, made up by people of the neighborhood, is sympathetic to María's predicament and reminds her that "en este país tener el pellejo prieto es una desgracia" [To have dark skin in this country is a misfortune] (*Medea*, 27).

María's poor self-esteem and worldview, based on the value system of the dominant group, induce her to pretend being a white middle-class lady and to despise her own speech, culture, and people.[16] Making a fool of herself and alienating herself from the members of her race, María constantly attempts to "whitewash" her speech, and treats people of color around her with cruelty, including Erundina, the black woman who raised her as her daughter, and Miss Amparo, the nanny of her children. In the opening scene, María mocks Erundina's slang and behavior:

> ¿Son esos los modales propios de tratar a una señora? Me has mentido, Erundina. Indudablemente no fuiste a un colegio de monjas. Tendré que vigilar la educación de mis hijos. . . . No quiero que se acostumbren a tanto desparpajo. Yo misma hago esfuerzos. (*La mira con desprecio.*) Hablamos idiomas distintos.

> [Is that the proper way to address a lady? You have lied to me, Erundina. Undoubtedly, you did not attend a Catholic school. I will have to watch my children's education. . . . I do not want them to grow used to such manners. I myself try very hard. (*María looks at her with contempt.*) We speak different languages.]
>
> (*Medea*, 16)

María's solution is to find and to reaffirm her identity, lost in the shadows of social prejudice. The mirror leitmotiv, introduced in the title, is the symbol of the assertion of the identity. In some Afro-Cuban religions, the mirror is employed to ascertain the whereabouts of a missing person.[17] In *Medea en el espejo*, Erundina repeatedly advises María that she should turn to the mirror for help: "Debes mirarte en él. . . . Recuerda quién eres, María" [You ought to look at yourself in it. . . . Remember who you are, María] (*Medea*, 14). The protagonist does not rectify her attitude in time, as Erundina forewarns (*Medea* 15), and goes on evading her image in the mirror, up to the point where only a violent act can set her free. The sacrifice of her children becomes an expiatory act that restores the lost order. It not only punishes Julián's betrayal but also María's ignominy, her shameful stand against her race and her people. In the final scene, the chorus, horrified by the murder of the children, encircles the heroine, chanting accusations. A deranged María engages in a frenetic dance, "reafirmando su posición en el mundo" [reaffirming her position in the universe] (*Medea*, 54), and utters a wild cry: "Soy Dios" [I am God] (*Medea*, 54). María's madness is the deus ex machina of the tragedy, the only possible way out after having stained her hands with the blood of her own children. However, considering the protagonist's purpose of asserting her identity, her final words connote her perception within the tragic scheme of the play: María's madness is revealing; it is the derangement of the visionary; metaphorically, she is God because she has created herself by finding and asserting her Afro-Cuban identity, taking charge of her existence and her destiny.

The use of Afro-Cuban music throughout *Medea en el espejo* is far from serving as a colorful folk element; it emerges on the stage as a theatrical sign with rich connotations.[18] The rhythms of the Cuban *son,* as well as the almost omnipresent beat of the drums, both function as deictic signs of the geographical and cultural context of the play. Within the world of the play, the music reminds the protagonist of her cultural heritage. When María finds out about Julián's wedding plans, the stage directions specify that the characters "comienzan a moverse rítmicamente. Esta escena debe mantener un ritmo de son" [start moving rhythmically. This scene must keep up the rhythm of the *son*] *(Medea,* 25). The frequent repetitions of certain phrases by the members of the chorus, which might seem monotonous to the reader, are charged with energy when performed to the beat of the Cuban *son.* Besides establishing the geographical, religious, and sociocultural context of the dramatic action, the music is reminiscent of the Afro-Cuban poetry, an intertextuality in *Medea en el espejo* noticed by José A. Escarpanter.[19] Afro-Cuban poetry, a literary trend originated in the 1930s, incorporated Afro-Caribbean music within its discourse as an element of self-assertion, adopting also its rebellious, or anti-establishment, tone.[20] The beat of the drums in slave plantations, which white people interpreted only as a sign of celebration or religious rite, at times communicated a message of self-assertion and of rebellion only understood by the blacks. In *Medea en el espejo,* the rebellious message transmitted by the "tam tam de tambores" [tam tam of the drums] *(Medea,* 47) goes unnoticed by Julián and Perico Piedra Fina. During the wedding festivities, Perico drinks eagerly the poisoned wine that María presented to him as a feigned sign of docility and submission. The stage directions suggest that the members of the chorus are aware—perhaps through the drums played in the background— of María's intentions since they remain on the alert and seem satisfied with Perico's remarks and movements as he drinks the potion *(Medea,* 43). When the poison takes effect, the chorus sings to the beat of the drums, rejoicing over Perico Piedra Fina's death *(Medea,* 46).

Other differentiating elements in *Medea en el espejo* are the motifs of the gossip and the *bachata,* which parody the seriousness of the tragedy. De la Campa asserts that gossip constitutes in itself one of the structural elements of the play.[21] In the play, the neighbors spread the rumor that María is "en la esquina de este solar sin nombre esperando el llamado de la sangre" [at the corner of the neighborhood, nameless, waiting for the call of the blood] (*Medea,* 25); the vox populi is well aware of María's situation, in which she finds herself marginalized, without an identity, waiting for the call of her race. The *bachata* motif becomes apparent in the behavior of the characters, who do not yield completely to the gravity of the tragedy. It also becomes evident when elements of the popular culture are introduced as theatrical devices to mock the tragic situation. When María demands to be told the whereabouts of Julián, Miss Amparo hesitates to reveal to her the rumors about Julián's pending wedding. This scene employs in a parodic fashion elements from melodrama and radio soaps, for example, the suspense created by incomplete phrases and stressed by the music:

> *María.* ¿Qué tiene que ver la mujer de Perico Piedra Fina en todo esto?
> *Srta.* Ella es la madre.
> *María.* ¿La madre de quién?
> *Srta.* De su hija.
> *María.* La hija, de qué madre.
> *Srta.* La hija de su madre.

> [*María.* What does Perico Piedra Fina's wife have to do with all this?
> *Miss.* She's the mother.
> *María.* Whose mother?
> *Miss.* Of her daughter.
> *María.* The daughter of what mother?
> *Miss.* The daughter of her mother.]

(Medea, 22)

At this point, when the truth is about to be exposed, "se oye como un suave rumor de maracas y claves" [one hears what seems the gentle murmur of maracas and *claves* (Afro-Caribbean percussion instrument)] (*Medea,* 23).

Outbursts of melodrama may be seen as a parody of the grandiloquent tone of the classical tragedy. In the first act, María announces to Erundina that she will no longer take care of the children; Erundina's reaction is unexpectedly comical:

> *Erundina.* Oye, María, no me hagas esta trastada.
> *María.* Ordenes estrictas.
> *Erundina. (En un ataque de histeria.)* Sabotaje. Sabotaje.

[*Erundina.* Listen, María, do not play this dirty trick on me.
María. Strict orders.
Erundina. (Hysterically.) Sabotage. Sabotage.]

(*Medea,* 17)

The *bachata* also emerges in the juxtaposition of contrasting speech modes (rhetorical grandiloquence and common speech/ slang) that simultaneously brings Triana's character closer to its Euripidian model and establishes a dissonant note that disrupts any illusion of affinity.[22] Before discovering Julián's betrayal, María has a feeling of an upcoming calamity:

María. Ah, infortunio. ¿Qué mal es el mío que los demás conociéndolo no se atreven a nombrar? ¿Qué mal, oh sombra de las sombras? ¿Cáncer o tuberculosis? *(Rechazando una horrible visión.)* Lepra. ¿Será eso lepra? ¿Mi cuerpo ha sido tocado por las llagas del diablo? Oh, lepra, lepra, lepra.

[*María.* Oh, misfortune. What kind of evil haunts me that people, knowing it, do not dare to name? What evil, oh shadow of the shadows? Cancer or tuberculosis? *(Repelling a horrible vision.)* Leprosy. Would it be leprosy? My body has been touched by the devil's sores? Oh, leprosy, leprosy, leprosy.]

(*Medea,* 19–20)

At the beginning of this speech, it appears that the character starts to grasp her existential dilemma, but María swings from the highflown language of the tragedy to melodramatic and ridiculous metaphors (illnesses) of her plight.

The contrast between the different speech modes not only mocks the tragic genre but also aims the parody at the text itself, which constitutes the best example of *bachata* in Triana's play. The parody of the canonical tragedy is implied in the stage directions describing María's behavior: "Jugando" [Joking]; "Tono melodramático" [Melodramatic tone]; "Exagerando" [Exaggerating]; "Solemne y ridícula al mismo tiempo" [Solemn and ridiculous at the same time] (*Medea,* 15, 18, 20, 21). These stage directions indicate how the actress performing the role should undermine the seriousness of the situation. Right after María finds out about Julián's wedding, the chorus enters for the first time to comment on the conflict. The Barber whispers, as if gossiping: "Caballero, que no se diga. Una tragedia. Lo que se llama una verdadera tragedia" [Sir, who would believe it! A tragedy. What you call a real tragedy] (*Medea,* 26). The Vendor of newspapers and lottery tickets hawks:

"Tragedia. Una tragedia. El 6,283, matrimonio que termina en tragedia. El 6,284, matrimonio que termina en sangre" [Tragedy. A tragedy. Number 6,283, marriage that ends in tragedy. Number 6,284, marriage that ends in bloodshed] (*Medea*, 26). The (self-) mockery in the text leads us to the metatheatrical character of *Medea en el espejo;* the strong metatheatrical effect of Triana's adaptation is reinforced by the audience's familiarity with Euripides' *Medea* and the intrusion of the parody within the tragic structure of the dramatic action.[23]

Self-reference is the metatheatrical device most used by Triana in *Medea en el espejo,* although other varieties of the metadramatic—the ceremony within the play, literary and real-life references, role playing within the role—function in the text as well. Most of the main characters (María, Erundina, Perico Piedra Fina) comment on the fictional nature of the dramatic action, thus altering the relationship established between the spectators and the text.[24] In the first scene of the play, María is consumed by the anguish caused by Julián's absence and fears the attitude of those around her:

> Tengo que actuar con cautela. Los demás intentan hacerme saltar. . . . Julián, Julián, Julián. Mi destino eres tú. *(Aparece Erundina por lateral izquierdo.)* Representaré. Me pondré a la altura de la circunstancias.

> [I have to act cautiously. Everybody is trying to pressure me. . . . Julián, Julián, Julián. You are my destiny. *(Erundina enters from the stage left.)* I'll perform. I'll manage to rise to the occasion.]
>
> (*Medea*, 13)

The protagonist initiates her "performance" revealing her intention to feign; as Dauster points out, "she does indeed put on a performance, feigning, like Hamlet, as part of a plan for revenge."[25] María realizes that her acts (feigned or not) should agree with the tone of the tragedy. Later on, she communicates to Erundina and Miss Amparo that "alguien ha organizado tremendo show con el objeto de destruirme" [someone has put on an amazing show with the objective of destroying me] (*Medea*, 19). The self-reference is equally supported by the characters' parodic remarks on the speech style or the melodramatic reaction of other characters. Richard Hornby states that self-reference "always has the effect of drastically realigning the audience's perception of the drama, forcing them to examine consciously the assumptions that lie behind and control their response to the world of the play."[26]

The intrusion of the parody, the incorporation of differentiating elements, and the metadramatic devices widen the textual rift between Euripides' play and Triana's; they also can be perceived as a metacritical answer to the hegemonic canon. In *Medea en el espejo* the transgression is not directed so much to Euripides' text, but rather to European theatrical conventions and expectations. The Cuban play transgresses the genre of classical tragedy using what Michael D. Bristol describes as the contamination of an official literary structure: the canonical text—in this case, Euripides' *Medea*—is "traversed, or 'contaminated,' by other 'texts' inscribed in the social life of the audience."[27] Among the popular "texts" incorporated by Triana in his rewriting of the classical myth are the parodic versions of the press, the melodrama and the radio soaps, the Afro-Cuban music and religion, and the farce *(teatro bufo)*. Bristol concludes that "the contamination—or to reverse ethical signs, the Carnivalization—of literature forces a dramatic text to 'speak up for the interests of its own times.'"[28]

The insertion of the character of Medea in the historical and cultural context of Latin America subtly exposes the perception of marginality of the playwright dealing with hegemonic conventions. One could argue that the examination of the cultural identity of a nation from the Third World through a First World (hegemonic) cultural artifact is contradictory. However, the rewriting of the classical myth from a revisionist perspective is perhaps a viable response to such discrepancy, not unlike the solution proposed by the play: María's first step toward the assertion of her identity is to acknowledge her otherness.

As a conclusion, I want to propose an analogy between María and the text of *Medea en el espejo*. The protagonist, at the moment of (self-) discovery, or anagnorisis, contemplates her image in the mirror and asserts: "Ahora caigo en la cuenta que mi destino no es Julián. . . . Tengo necesidad de ser, de ser eternamente" [Now I realize that Julián is not my destiny. . . . I feel the need to be, to be eternally] *(Medea,* 48). Following her self-assertion, she immerses herself in a violent act that symbolically restores her lost identity. Triana's text, a play belonging to a marginalized theatrical corpus, asserts its Latin American identity through subversive or transgressive devices, such as the parody and the carnivalization, aimed at a canonical text. The differentiating elements in *Medea en el espejo*, which can be found in other Latin American plays that recreate classical myths, help us go beyond the masks of European conventions, serving as a mirror that reveals the true face of Latin American dramaturgy.

Notes

1. Costa Palamides, "Mito griego y teatro latinoamericano del siglo XX," *Primer Acto,* no. 229 (1989), 57.

2. Ibid., 58.

3. José A. Escarpanter, Introducción, in José Triana, *Medea en el espejo. La noche de los asesinos. Palabras comunes* (Madrid: Verbum, 1991), 9.

4. Frank N. Dauster, "The Game of Chance: The Theater of José Triana," in *Dramatists in Revolt: The New Latin American Theater,* ed. Leon F. Lyday and George W. Woodyard (Austin: University of Texas Press, 1977), 167.

5. George Woodyard, "José Triana," in *Nueve dramaturgos hispanoamericanos,* ed. Frank Dauster, Leon Lyday, and George Woodyard, 3 vols. (Ottawa: Girol, 1983), 1:134.

6. Dauster, "Game of Chance," 183.

7. Diana Taylor, *Theatre of Crisis: Drama and Politics in Latin America* (Lexington: The University Press of Kentucky, 1991), 66.

8. Frank Dauster, *Historia del tetro hispanoamericano (siglos XIX y XX)* (Mexico: Ediciones de Andrea, 1973), 130.

9. Euripides, *The Plays of Euripides,* ed. Ernest Rhys (New York: Dutton, 1917), 1:71.

10. Osvaldo Obregón, "Pervivencia de mitos griegos en obras dramáticas hispanoamericanas contemporáneas," in *Permanences, emergences et résurgences culturelles dans le monde ibérique et ibero-americain. Actes du XVIe Congrès National de la Societé des Hispanistes Français, 15–17 Mars 1980* (Aix-en-Provence: Centre Aixois de Recherches Hispaniques, Université de Provence, 1981), 220.

11. Juan Villegas, "La especificidad del discurso crítico sobre el teatro hispanoamericano," *Gestos* 1, no. 2 (1986):67. For an in-depth discussion on the specificity of Spanish and Spanish American critical and theatrical discourses, see Juan Villegas, *Ideología y discurso crítico sobre el teatro de España y América Latina* (Minneapolis: The Prisma Institute, 1988).

12. Román V. de la Campa, *José Triana: Ritualización de la sociedad cubana* (Madrid: Institute for the Study of Ideologies and Literature, 1979), 55; Frank Dauster, *Ensayos sobre teatro hispanoamericano* (Mexico: Sep-Setentas, 1975), 15; Frank Dauster, "Triana, Felipe, Brene: Tres visiones de una realidad," in *En busca de una imagen: Ensayos críticos sobre Griselda Gambaro y José Triana,* ed. Diana Taylor (Ottawa: Girol, 1989), 134; Escarpanter, Introducción, 10.

13. Villegas, "La especificidad," 67.

14. See Diana Taylor, "Entrevista con José Triana," in *En busca de una imagen,* 115–23, for the playwright's comments on his attack on racism in some of his texts, including *Medea en el espejo.*

15. José Triana, *Medea en el espejo,* in *El parque de la fraternidad* (Havana: Unión, 1962), 30. Hereafter *Medea,* cited in the text. All English translations of the play are mine.

16. De la Campa, *José Triana,* 51.

17. Fernando Ortiz, *Los negros brujos,* prologue by Alberto N. Pamies (Miami, Fla.: Universal, 1973), 113.

18. I adopt Martin Esslin's definition of theatrical signs. See Esslin's *The Field of Drama: How the Signs of Drama Create Meaning on Stage & Screen* (New York: Methuen, 1987).

19. Escarpanter, Introducción, 10.

20. See Eloise Y. Spicer's "The Blues and the Son: Reflections of Black Self-Assertion in the Poetry of Langston Hughes and Nicolás Guillén," *The Langston Hughes Review* 3, no. 1 (1984):1–12, for an analysis of the significance of the drums in Guillén's poetry. Unlikely a coincidence, Triana's employment of the Cuban *son* in his play recalls the title of one of the most important works of Afro-Cuban poetry, *Motivos de son* (1930) by Guillén.

21. De la Campa, *José Triana*, 47.

22. Dauster, "Game of Chance," 171.

23. See Richard Hornby, *Drama, Metadrama, and Perception* (Lewisburg, Pa.: Bucknell University Press, 1986), for a detailed discussion of the concept of metadrama and its varieties.

24. Ibid., 105.

25. Dauster, "Game of Chance," 171.

26. Hornby, *Drama*, 117.

27. Michael D. Bristol, *Carnival and Theater: Plebeian Culture and the Structure of Authority in Renaissance England* (New York: Routledge, 1989), 160.

28. Ibid.